Justification and Sanctification

FOUNDATIONS FOR FAITH

General editor: Peter Toon

FOUNDATIONS FOR FAITH

Justification and Sanctification

Peter Toon

Crossway Books • Westchester, Illinois
A division of Good News Publishers

Copyright © 1983 by Peter Toon
First published by Marshall Morgan & Scott and Crossway Books, 1983
All rights reserved
Printed in the United States of America for
Crossway Books, 9825 W. Roosevelt Rd., Westchester, Illinois 60153
ISBN 0-89107-288-8
and
Marshall Morgan & Scott, 1 Bath Street, London ECIV 9LB
ISBN 0 551 01088 6

Bible quotations from the New International Version,
copyright © 1978 by the New York
International Bible Society, are used
by permission of Zondervan Bible Publishers.

For
The Right Reverend
John Waine,
Bishop of the diocese of
St. Edmunsbury and Ipswich, England

CONTENTS

PREFACE

It has been and remains commonplace for Protestants to describe the Christian life in terms of justification by faith or justification and sanctification. This tradition developed in the early decades of the Reformation, found its way into the Protestant catechisms and confessions of faith and became a part of the distinctively Protestant language of salvation.

This short study, which aims only to introduce the subject of justification and sanctification, is divided into three parts. First of all there is an examination of the meaning of righteousness/justice (justification) and holiness (sanctification) in the sacred Scriptures. Such an examination does not, of course, represent a comprehensive study of all that is said of the Christian life in the New Testament. Its purpose is to enable the reader to be in a position to begin to evaluate the various doctrines of justification which have emerged in the Church over the centuries.

The second part presents the history of the doctrine of justification and its relation to sanctification. There is careful selection so that the reader can see how the Protestant doctrine is related to the earlier patristic and medieval teaching and where it differs from the dogma promulgated by the Roman Catholic Council of Trent. In the final part examples of recent Protestant and Roman Catholic expositions of the doctrine are noticed.

This book will have served its purpose if it encourages the reader to pursue further study of the biblical, historical or contemporary material. The time seems ripe for the further explication of this area of doctrine in the dialogue between denominations as well as its application to the pastoral ministry of the churches and the life of individual Christians.

Quotations from the Bible are taken from the *New International Version,* except where it is otherwise indicated.

I regret the completion of this book before release of the final volume in the important dialogue between American Lutheran and Roman Catholic scholars, which will deal with justification. However, I am happy to report that through the kindness of Dr. John Reumann I was allowed to see in prepublication form his valuable book, *"Righteousness" in the New Testament: Justification in the Lutheran-Catholic Dialogue* (1983), which incorporates material presented in the scriptural studies in the dialogue. Further, I need to thank Dr. A. E. McGrath for his help and to state that we look forward to seeing his detailed history of the doctrine of justification presented in three volumes (*Iustitia Dei: A History of the Christian Doctrine of Justification,* James Clarke, Cambridge).

Finally I would like to dedicate this book to the Right Reverend John Waine, Bishop of St. Edmunsbury and Ipswich. He has made me most welcome in his diocese and has honored me by describing me as his "theological consultant."

Peter Toon
November 1982

Part 1: Biblical

1 INTRODUCTION

We are all familiar with Jesus' parable about the Pharisee and the tax-collector who worked for the occupying forces, the Romans (Luke 18). They both went to pray in the Temple at Jerusalem. The Pharisee, proud of his religious achievements, thanked God for his piety and morality. In contrast, the tax-collector, shunned by contemporary Jewish religious society, prayed that God would have pity upon him as a sinner. Jesus concluded that it was the tax-collector and not the Pharisee who was *dedikaiōmenos* (perfect passive from *dikaioō*)—that is, in right relationship with the Lord when he went home from the Temple. Such a story is alarming, raising not only basic questions about religious practice and duty, but also the fundamental question about how a human being, even a devout human being, is to have a right relationship with God, our Creator and Redeemer. It is not surprising that during times of profound religious and spiritual searching (e.g., the Protestant Reformation) the idea of justification by faith is prominent.

The Greek word *dedikaiōmenos* in Luke 18:14 can be translated in a variety of ways: "justified" (KJV/AV; RV; RSV), "justified before God" (NIV), "acquitted of sins" (NEB), "at rights with God" (JB), and "in the right with God" (TEV). In English we have an old tradition of translating *dikaioō* as "to justify." Yet when the noun *dikaiosunē* occurs, as in Matthew 6:33, we have an equally old tradition of translating it as "righteousness" (KJV/AV, RV) with a modern rendering of "justice" (NEB). In translating into English words of the *dikaio*-stem, scholars have used the nouns "justice" and "righteousness," the adjectives "just" and "righteous," and the verbs "to justice," "to justify" and "to rightwise." Of these verbs, "to justice" and "to rightwise" ceased to be generally used in the sixteenth century, leaving only "to justify." This means that unless we revive the verb "to rightwise," there is now no verb from the *right*-stem to function as a synonym of "to justify." We speak of the gospel as revealing the righteousness of God and declaring that the ungodly are justified. This raises the further problem of whether *dikaioō* means either to declare righteous/just or to make righteous/just. Does our English word "justify" mean to *declare* just or to *make* just?

The Greek translators of the Old Testament generally used *dikaioō* to translate the Hebrew root *ṣdq*. What is the principal concept that is found in the contexts in which this word occurs? Scholars agree that this concept relates to the administration of justice within the covenant which God made with his elect people, the Israelites. However, it pictures an ancient Hebrew and not a modern Western law court. *Dikaioō* refers to the laws of the land and the tradition of their interpretation. In fact, there is no word in Old Testament Hebrew which literally means "a court." The word that is used is literally translated as "the gate of the city," for that was the ancient place, along with the central religious sanctuary, where a "court" met. The judge (the King or an elder) heard the statements of the accuser and the accused, called and heard witnesses, and then gave his judgment (see e.g., 2 Samuel 15:1-6; 1 Kings 3:16ff.). Justification is the verdict of the judge in favor of one party or another; it is more than mere aquittal, for it carries the definite idea of actually being in the right and thus "righteous."

Scholars refer to this meaning of *ṣdq* and *diakaioō* as forensic, which simply indicates that it has to do with a court of law. To assert that the basic meaning is forensic is not to deny that the forensic often easily moves over in the Old Testament into the ethical, referring to the life of faith/faithfulness of members of God's covenant people. We must expect a certain fluidity in ancient words and concepts.

As the Bible has been interpreted in the history of the Church, the basic forensic idea of righteousness/justice has not always been fully appreciated. Sometimes it has not been known or taken seriously, and the ethical idea has been prominent. Thus *dikaioō* and its Latin equivalent *justificare* were for many centuries understood in the West as primarily ethical, meaning "to make righteous." At other times, particularly in Protestant use of the Bible, the forensic idea of declaratory righteousness was heightened through the use not of a picture of justice at the gate of the city but rather in a Roman or Western court of law. Thus, though the forensic idea was preserved, it was exaggerated and separated wholly from the ethical. Let's look deeper at these topics.

1

The basic Hebrew verb *ṣdq* means "to be righteous" and in its hiphil stem means "to declare to be in the right." About 90 percent of the 500 or so occurrences of words from the root *ṣdq* in the Hebrew Bible are rendered in the Septuagint by words from the root *dikaioō*. These 500 or so occurrences are found mostly in the books of Psalms, Proverbs, Isaiah and Ezekiel. *Ṣdq* is used both of God and human beings, primarily in the forensic sense but sometimes with an ethical emphasis.[1]

2

The Lord is seen as the righteous one who acts justly. He is the just judge who judges righteously. His character is clear to all. "From the ends of the earth we hear singing: 'Glory to the Righteous One' " (Isa. 24:16). What Jeremiah heard from Heaven is true: "I am the LORD, who exercises kindness, justice and righteousness on earth, for in these I delight" (9:24). The psalmist had to sing: "Righteousness and justice are the foundation of your throne; love and faithfulness go before you" (89:14). When psalmist and prophet celebrated the *ṣedeq* of their Lord, they were not thinking of what we call distributive justice. Rather, they were praising his attitude and activity in perfectly maintaining his side of the gracious covenant which he made with the people of Israel.

Yahweh, the LORD, judge of the whole world, acts in *ṣedeq* toward Israel, upholding the right; but that right is determined by his own free choice of Abraham and descendants as his elect people. Thus the righteousness/justice of the Lord can both chastise Israel (Lam. 1:8) and deliver from trouble, oppression and disaster (Ps. 68; 103:6). It can also mean salvation for Israel and destruction of her enemies (Ps. 58:10, 11; Hab. 3:12, 13; Mal. 4:1-3), as well as punishment for some Israelites and vindication for others (Ps. 51:4; 116:5, 6; 146:7, 8).

The forensic is seen when the prophets represent the activity of God's *ṣedeq* in the picture of a court where the judge faces the accused and passes sentence after hearing and reviewing the evidence. The Lord is the judge, and Israel is the party who is accused and then condemned by God according to the covenant relationship which exists between them. Perhaps the best-known of these prophetic pictures is found in Micah 6:1-8 (but see also Isaiah 1:2-9 and Jeremiah 2:4-13).

> Hear, O mountains, the LORD'S accusation;
>   listen, you everlasting foundations of the earth.
> For the LORD has a case against his people;
>   he is lodging a charge against Israel.

The Lord as judge brings forth the accusation, and the terms of reference are the basic conditions of the covenant. God's righteousness requires that he accuse and chastise Israel in order to restore the people to the right relationship required by their covenant. What he looks for in Israel is behavior that reflects the right relationship with himself: "And what does the LORD require of you? To act justly and to love mercy and to walk humbly with your God" (6:8). In this way the forensic and ethical are united.

Since Israel appealed to the Lord as righteous when they looked for deliverance from all kinds of troubles and enemies, it is not surprising that *ṣedeq* came to mean *salvation*. This is especially so in the latter part of the book of Isaiah where God's future saving action on behalf of his people is presented: "Listen to me, you stubborn-hearted, you who are far from righteousness. I am bringing my righteousness near; it is not far away; and my salvation will not be delayed" (46:12, 13). Where the NIV has "righteousness" the RSV has "deliverance"—"I bring near my deliverance." A similar function of God's *ṣedeq* as deliverance (RSV) is found in 51:5: "My righteousness draws near speedily, my salvation is on the way, and my arm will bring justice to the nations." In this context, to speak of God's righteousness is to speak of good news, which makes us think of Paul's connection of righteousness and good news in Romans 1:16, 17.

3

God's covenant people are to be like him. He is righteous; so they are to be righteous. But their righteousness is dependent upon and proceeds from his. When God called Abram and told him of his plans for the future, what he wanted to see in Abram was faith and trust accompanied by loving obedience. God set in motion a relationship, and what was needed as foundational at the beginning and forever was faith, faith in the God who made and keeps his promise. "Abram believed the LORD, and he credited it to Abram as righteousness" (Gen. 15:6). Here the Lord as judge places Abram in the right in terms of their covenantal relationship. Later God said: "I have chosen Abraham, so that he will direct his children and his household after him to keep the way of the LORD by doing what is right and just, so that the LORD will bring about for Abraham what he has promised him" (18:19). A right relationship with God required that Abraham do what is "right and just"; the forensic and the ethical cannot be separated.

The king of Israel, as the Lord's anointed one, was also to set an example of righteousness in the way that he created, maintained and restored right relationships within his people. Psalm 72 speaks of Solomon and the gift of righteousness given to him so that he would act righteously.

> Endow the king with your justice, O God,
>   the royal son with your righteousness.
> He will judge your people in righteousness,
>   your afflicted ones with justice.
> The mountains will bring prosperity to the people,
>   the hills the fruit of righteousness.
> He will defend the afflicted among the people
>   and save the children of the needy;
> He will crush the oppressor. (vv. 1-4)

Here there is great emphasis (as in Isaiah 11:4) on justice/righteousness.

Bearing this in mind, it is not surprising that faithful Israelites who were in a state of affliction or oppression were actually called "righteous" as they looked for vindication from their Lord. They are also called "the poor," meaning "the humble poor." In fact, God's judgments are always favorable for the oppressed, the hungry, the alien and the prisoner as well as the widow and the fatherless (see Amos 2:6ff.).

> He upholds the cause of the oppressed
> and gives food to the hungry.
> The LORD sets prisoners free,
> the LORD gives sight to the blind,
> the LORD lifts up those who are bowed down,
> the LORD loves the righteous.
> The LORD watches over the alien
> and sustains the fatherless and the widow,
> but he frustrates the ways of the wicked. (Ps. 146:7-9)

God decides in favor of the needy and declares him to be in the right. And this example is to be followed by his covenant people.

In Israel "righteous" referred primarily to one who lived faithfully as a member of the covenant people. Those who lived in faith and faithfulness as the Lord required were righteous, whether in riches or poverty, in their own land or in exile. The truly pious and righteous man also recognized that he was a sinner and so made full use of the means God had provided for atonement and remission of sin. This association of a consciousness of sin and righteousness occurs, for example, in Psalm 143. "No one living is righteous before you [the LORD]" (v. 2) is a way of saying that no pious Israelite is righteous all the time, for he always needs provision for the blotting out of his sins through prayer and sacrifice.

Though he recognizes his sin, the psalmist is also confident that God, the Righteous One, will preserve his life, bring him out of trouble, silence his enemies, hear his prayers and vindicate him. The psalmist believed that God had given him a righteous verdict because he had put his trust in the Lord—"I have put my trust in you" (v. 8). The prophet Habakkuk later put it this way: "The righteous will live by his faith (faithfulness)" (2:4).

Before any psalms were written or Abraham had been called out of Ur of the Chaldees, God had said of Noah that he was "a righteous man, blameless among the people of his time, and he walked with God" (Gen. 6:9). Here the ethical import of righteousness is prominent, as it is also in Psalm 15. There, in answer to the question, "Lord, who may dwell in your sanctuary (i.e., at Jerusalem)?," the following reply is provided:

> He whose walk is blameless and who does what is righteous,
> who speaks the truth from his heart

and has no slander on his tongue,
who does his neighbor no wrong
and casts no slur on his fellow man,
who despises a vile man but honors those who fear the LORD,
who keeps his oath even when it hurts,
who lends his money without usury
and does not accept a bribe against the innocent. (vv. 2-5)

The meaning is clear. God expects those who are within the covenant, and who on this basis have been declared to be in a right relationship with him, to live as children of the righteous Lord.

In Ezekiel 18:5-9 there is a striking and impressive picture of a righteous man who exercises his individual responsibility to do God's will as a member of God's covenant people. "He follows my decrees and faithfully keeps my laws. That man is righteous; he will surely live, declares the Sovereign LORD" (18:9). Where a mistake could be made, and in fact was made in later Judaism, was to think that God's declaration of righteousness was dependent upon an individual Jew's meticulous fulfillment of the laws within the covenant made with Moses on Mount Sinai. Actually, righteousness as an ethical quality of blamelessness came as a result of God's declaration of a right standing before him within his covenant of grace, and not the opposite way around. The Pharisee in Luke 18 represents the way in which the whole pursuit of righteousness can go wrong. He stopped looking to the Lord as the giver of righteousness and concentrated on seeking to achieve righteousness to present to the Lord at the end of his life.

The key to understanding *ṣdq* is to think of relationships. "There is absolutely no concept in the Old Testament," wrote the German Gerhard von Rad, "with so central a significance for all the relationships of human life as that of *ṣdq*. It is the standard not only for man's relationship with God, but also for his relationship to his fellows, reaching right down to . . . the animals and to his natural environment."[2] E. R. Achtemeier has written: "Righteousness is in the Old Testament the fulfillment of the demands of a relationship, whether that relationship be with men or with God. Each man is set within a multitude of relationships: king with people, judge with complainants, priests with worshippers, common man with family, tribesman with community, community with resident alien and poor, all with God. And each of these relationships brings with it specific demands, the fulfillment of which constitutes righteousness. The demands may differ from relationship to relationship; righteousness in one situation may be unrighteousness in another. Further, there is no norm of righteousness outside the relationship itself. When God or man fulfills the conditions imposed upon him by a relationship, he is, in Old Testament terms, righteous."[3]

The story of the Old Testament is, however, a story of the failure of men to be righteous and of God's faithfulness in righteousness. The

God of grace intervenes on behalf of his people to declare them in the right before himself and the world. So the way is prepared for the further righteous activity of God in Jesus Christ, the Righteous One, by whom the gift of righteousness is offered to the whole world in his gospel.

2 RIGHTEOUSNESS ACCORDING TO PAUL

The Gentiles were not, in one sense, a part of the covenants that God made with Abraham, Moses and David in the Old Testament. Yet the gospel of God "regarding his Son . . . Jesus Christ our Lord" (Rom. 1:2-4) was meant to be heard and received by them. God intended that they should become members of the new covenant, prophesied by Jeremiah (31:31ff.) and inaugurated by the blood of Jesus (Matt. 26:28). Through Jesus, the Savior, they would be included in the original covenant of grace that God made with Abraham and his descendants (Gen. 12:1-3).

But must they become converts to Judaism and join the historical Israel of God as proselytes in order to benefit from the gospel of God? Were conditions other than repentance and faith required of them? How was a right relationship created between Gentile sinners and the Lord, the God of Abraham and Moses? Paul's answer to these and related questions is found in the doctrine of justification by faith. Both Jews and Gentiles have a right relationship with God the Father through faith in Jesus, the Christ, who died for their sins and rose for their justification (Rom. 4:25). We are justified by faith through the grace of God apart from the Law of Moses.

The first substantial presentation of this doctrine of justification by faith alone occurs in the letter to the churches of Galatia, while the second, and theologically more developed, is found in the letter to the church in Rome. As we would expect, there are also important brief references in other letters—for example, Philippians 3:9-11 and Titus 3:3-7.

Let us be clear on one point. Justification by faith is not the actual message of the gospel preached to the heathen by Paul. Rather, it is an explanation of how the gospel is effective based on the great Old Testament themes of the righteousness of God and human faith.[1]

The Letter to Galatia[2]

Paul's letter to the churches in Galatia is brief, and it is advisable to read it through several times before ascertaining what it has to say about righteousness. Further, to appreciate Paul's teaching on this topic it is useful to note how the theme of righteousness was being used in primitive Christian teaching before Paul wrote his letter and also the basic elements of Paul's actual preaching to the heathen in Galatia. Since there are several very early Jewish-Christian formulations or confessions of faith embedded in parts of the New Testament, it is possible by looking at these to notice how righteousness was then understood.[3] If we take 1 Peter 3:18 and 1 Timothy 3:16 to be such formulations, then we notice that the use of the righteousness theme is Christological. Jesus is the Righteous One who died for the sins of the unrighteous and then was vindicated/justified by the Father in his exaltation into Heaven. Only at 1 Corinthians 6:11 do we encounter in a pre-Pauline formulation a reference to the justification of human beings: "But you were washed, you were sanctified, you were justified in the name of the Lord Jesus Christ and by the Spirit of our God." All the verbs are in the passive voice. The first may refer to baptism, while the other two are complementary ways of understanding the gracious work of God for and in believers, using familiar Old Testament themes of holiness and righteousness. To look for too precise a meaning of either term at this early stage in the life of the young Church would be a mistake. But here was something on which Paul could and did build.

The elements of Paul's good news for Galatia have to be deduced from the contents of his letter, the nature of the society of the region, and our general knowledge of early Christian proclamation. Fundamental to the good news was that there is one God, who revealed himself in days past to the people of Israel. He is not a tribal deity like the lords and gods known in the towns and cities of Asia Minor; he is the living and universal Lord. As the one and only living Lord, he desires, initiates and makes possible for human beings actual communion and fellowship with himself. This gracious activity of God is made a reality through Jesus of Nazareth who, though the Jews' Messiah, is also the Savior of all peoples. He died for the sins of the whole world, Jews and Gentiles, and rose victorious over death, sin and Hades. Therefore people of every race, social class and nation are called to believe in Jesus, the universal Savior and Lord, who is alive forevermore. In and through him salvation is freely given by God to each person who is ready to receive it, turning from idols and sin to serve the living Lord. Salvation from God includes the call to a new life within the community of the disciples of Jesus, with goals set by him and achieved by power from his Spirit. This outlines the message that Paul preached. We must emphasize that the apostle made no reference to a need to obey any of the requirements of the Law of Moses. The gospel he preached was a gospel concerning Christ and Christ alone.

Paul's teaching on justification/righteousness by faith undergirded the message of salvation and hope he had proclaimed in Galatia. Obviously he had thought about all this before, but he put it into writing because of the sinister effect certain false teachers were having on the churches he had founded. "I am astonished," he wrote, "that you are so quickly deserting the one who called you by the grace of Christ and are turning to a different gospel—which is really no gospel at all" (1:6). We know little about those who provided this false gospel except that they were probably Jews who accepted Jesus of Nazareth as the Messiah of Israel and Savior of the world. But they differed from Paul in what they added to the basic confession of faith in Jesus. They said something like this: "What Paul told you is fine, but it is not the whole story. He omitted to tell you to complete your obedience to the God and Father of our Lord Jesus by submitting (as Gentiles have always done) to the basic requirements of the Law of Moses. In particular, this means that all males must be circumcised. Further, both male and female must obey the dietary regulations and keep the Sabbath and Feast days." In effect they were saying that Jesus, the Christ, is not a complete Savior: Gentile believers not only need Christ to be put in the right with God but also the Law of Moses for their full acceptance with God.

These Judaizers, as they are usually called, had a different view of justification than the non-Christian, orthodox Jews of their time. Pious, orthodox Jews looked forward to being declared in the right by God at the Last Judgment because as members of God's covenant they had provided meticulous obedience to the Law of Moses through their lives. The Christian Judaizers saw the need for and the importance of the expiatory death of Jesus as Messiah for their sins. They believed that through Jesus, the Righteous One, they were already sanctified and justified (1 Cor. 6:11). Yet, to be guaranteed full acceptance by God at the Last Judgment, they believed, they and all Christians—Jew and Gentile alike—had to practice Christian discipleship within the demands of the Law of Moses.

Paul believed that the Judaizers were corrupting the gospel of God. In his own teaching to the churches of Galatia he narrated an account of an incident involving Peter, God's apostle to the Jews. At Antioch, the church from which Paul had begun his apostolic labors, Peter joined in the fellowship around the meal table and at the Lord's Table and quite happily, as a Jew and contrary to common Jewish practice, actually ate with Gentiles who were uncircumcised members of the church (2:11-14). He Hellenized harmoniously until, on receipt of certain information from Jerusalem, he not only ceased to fellowship with Gentile Christians but began to actively persuade those Gentiles to submit to circumcision and other requirements of the Law. Even Barnabas, who had been Paul's faithful companion in the Gentile mission of the church, was persuaded to follow Peter. Whatever were Peter's reasons, Paul was shocked and rebuked him. The basis of Paul's evangelism had been that Gentiles are saved by grace and are under no obligation whatsoever to become Jewish proselytes.

Therefore, seeing that the gospel of God as it had been revealed to him by the Lord Jesus (Acts 9) was on trial, Paul addressed some forceful words to Peter and his companions and then offered this profound teaching (using four words of the *dikaio*-stem).

> We who are Jews by birth and not "Gentile sinners" know that a man is not justified by observing the law, but by faith in Jesus Christ. So we, too, have put our faith in Christ Jesus that we may be justified by faith in Christ and not by observing the law, because by observing the law no one will be justified. If, while we seek to be justified in Christ, it becomes evident that we ourselves are sinners, does that mean that Christ promotes sin? Absolutely not! If I rebuild what I destroyed, I prove that I am a lawbreaker. (2:15-18)

Both Peter and Paul were circumcised Jews, and so members of the covenant God made with Moses (Ex. 19ff.). They were not "Gentile sinners" who had no revelation of God and his will. Further, as Christians the two apostles were in a right relationship with God the Father through Jesus Christ the Lord, a relationship begun when they believed and received the gospel of God. They were accepted by God and placed in a right relationship with him not because of their commitment to the Law of Moses but through the grace of God in Jesus Christ, to which they responded in faith.

Perhaps verse 16b needs unpacking. Paul is saying, "We Jews are convinced that a human being needs to be accepted and declared righteous by God at the Last Judgment. Further, as Jews we are convinced that such acceptance will never be achieved by our fulfillment of the rules and ordinances of the Law. Instead we have come to see that acceptance by God occurs now—in anticipation of acceptance at the Last Judgment—through what Jesus Christ has achieved for us. The gift of salvation, provided in and through Jesus, we gratefully accept in faith, gaining thereby a right relationship with God our Father through our Lord Jesus Christ."

Verse 17 refers to the breaking of Jewish law and custom concerning eating with Gentiles, who are Christians but uncircumcised. The righteousness of God provided in Christ places Jews and Gentiles on the same footing before God, the judge of all. Therefore, actions truly taken within the Christian fellowship on the basis of this gift of righteousness in Christ cannot be sinful, for it is impossible for Christ to be the agent or initiator of sin. In contrast, however, to deny the unity of Jew and Gentile in Christ through the gift of the one righteousness and to act on the old basis of division based on the Law is in fact to become a sinner, even a sinner against Christ himself. This was what

Peter had done. He should have known that once a Jew is in Christ there is no return to the old ways of Jewish isolationism.

There is no escape from the fact that justification by faith means a changed life. This is emphasized in the "autobiographical" section of Paul's letter (2:19-21). Actually though, the use of the first person singular is not to be taken as though it were Paul's personal experience. It is a literary device by which Paul speaks for all those whom God justifies and accepts as his children. Four truths are set forth.

First of all, *"through the law I died to the law so that I might live for God"* (v. 19). Paul sees the function of the Law as (1) that which separated Jew and Gentile and prevented Gentiles from coming to God except as proselytes; and (2) that which was a temporary measure, preparing for the advent of the Messiah, but is now finished. Set free from the Law by Christ, the Christian can truly live for God, being empowered by the indwelling Spirit of Christ.

Secondly, *"I have been crucified with Christ"* (v. 20). The death of Christ by crucifixion was not merely the death of a man; it was the death of the Representative Man, with the result that his death is also the death of all who are united to him within the new covenant. The sinful self of each believer was crucified and put to death on the cross.

So, thirdly, *"I no longer live, but Christ lives in me"* (v. 20). The "I" here is the ego of man, seen as the root of evil passions and desires (cf. 5:24). This center of personal existence in the believer has been crucified in and with Christ. The new center of motivation and freedom within the justified believer is the living Christ—the exalted Christ who now acts in and by the Spirit.

Finally, *"the life I live in the body, I live by faith in the Son of God, who loved me and gave himself for me"* (v. 20). The Christian life of the justified believer is based on faith and centered on Christ. There is no room in it for subjection to the Law of Moses.

Was such teaching a denial of God's revelation recorded in the Old Testament? Surely Abraham was justified by God because he was a circumcised and faithful servant of God! Paul's reply was that Abraham is the example, *par excellence,* of justification by faith.

> Consider Abraham: "He believed God, and it was credited to him as righteousness." Understand, then, that those who believe are children of Abraham. The Scripture foresaw that God would justify the Gentiles by faith, and announced the gospel in advance to Abraham: "All nations will be blessed through you." So those who have faith are blessed along with Abraham, the man of faith. (3:6-9)

Perhaps the key statement here is the quotation, "All peoples on earth will be blessed through you" (Gen. 12:3). Abraham is presented not only as the great example of a man justified by faith (Genesis 15:6 is quoted in v. 6), but also as the one to whom the Lord made the momentous promise which became the basis of God's further gracious activity in bringing salvation and justification to the Gentiles. So the story of justification by faith actually begins with the Lord himself keeping faith and being faithful to the promise made to Abraham. It reaches its climax in Jesus, the Messiah, who also kept faith with the Father in life and sacrificial death. The exalted Lord Jesus is the personal embodiment of the ancient promise, which means that all who are united to him by faith are justified, even as Abraham was justified by faith.

The gift of a right relationship with God, promised to Jews and Gentiles in the covenant made with Abraham, is available everywhere and for all because Jesus Christ lives forevermore and is present by his Spirit wherever the gospel of God is proclaimed. What Paul wanted to establish beyond all doubt and in answer to all Judaizing was that salvation is wholly the gift of God. God made the promise, and God has fulfilled the promise. God is righteous, and he alone gives the gift of righteousness. Whatever human beings do in terms of believing and trusting, following and obeying, is only response to what is already wholly provided in the exalted Lord Jesus and the omnipresent Spirit.

If God always intended that a right relationship with him was by faith, why did he give the Law of Moses? Paul answers that before the era of faith arrived,

> we were held prisoners by the law, locked up until faith should be revealed. So the law was put in charge to lead us to Christ that we might be justified by faith. Now that faith is come, we are no longer under the supervision of the law. (3:23-25)

The function of the Law before the era of faith (which came with the exaltation of Jesus into Heaven) was like that of a slave carefully guiding and protecting his master's child on the way home from school. He prevented the child from going anywhere or doing anything other than what the master had decreed. He was a repressive custodian. But with the arrival of the era of faith there is no need for such an overseer. The children of God, as true believers, are led by the indwelling Spirit of Christ to love, trust and obey their heavenly Father and their Lord and Savior, Jesus Christ. For them, the Law of Moses as a custodian or guide is no longer necessary because they belong to Christ and live under his Lordship in the power of his Spirit.

It is clear from those parts of the letter we have examined that justification by faith as a right relationship with God in Christ does not, indeed cannot, exist in isolation from a life directed by the Spirit of Christ. The effectual word of the Lord (Gen. 12:1-3; Isa. 55:10, 11) which places the believer in a right relationship with his God also puts him into the body of Christ (3:28) and gives him the gift of freedom, which is a freedom to love others and to serve them (5:1). This same effectual word and promise of the Lord produces hope that on the basis of the justification revealed in the gospel there will be full and complete justification in the life to come: "By faith we eagerly await through the Spirit the righteousness for which we hope" (5:5). The Christian lives by faith but the expression of his life is in terms of love for others: "the only thing that counts is faith expressing itself through love" (5:6). Justification as a right standing before and relationship with God has inevitable consequences for daily life. As we noticed in the psalms of ancient Israel, he who is righteous before God will also be righteous with and before human beings.

The Letter to Rome[4]

Why did Paul write such a long letter to a church he had not founded? And why did he present such deep theology in it? We know that he wanted to extend the preaching of the gospel to Spain and hoped that the Christians in Rome would assist him in this task (15:24). He explained to them the dynamics of his teaching so as to gain their confidence. Rome was the capital of the civilized world, and it was important that the church there should be strong in the faith so it could be for the western Mediterranean and other areas what Antioch had been for the east (Acts 13). It is also probable that Paul wanted to produce for the churches in the Roman Empire a handbook of the gospel of God which he and others proclaimed. The need to write to Rome provided the opportunity to produce this, and it is probable that copies were made to use in other churches.

In harmony with his teaching to the Galatian churches, Paul's explanation to the Roman Christians of how the gospel of Christ is effective in bringing God's salvation to mankind is in terms of God's righteousness. After his opening remarks he declares that "in the gospel a righteousness from God is revealed, a righteousness that is by faith from first to last . . ." (1:17). Here are the twin themes of righteousness and faith. Considering this initial statement, the presence of sixty-three words from the *dikaio*-stem in the letter, and its general structure and content, righteousness or justification may be seen as its unifying or overarching theme.

After the initial declaration of the revelation of God's righteousness, the long section of 1:18—3:20 may be seen as a statement of the solemn fact that in the light of the gospel of God all people—without any exceptions—are sinners. No human person is reckoned as righteous by God except on the basis of personal faith. Then, in the supremely important paragraph of 3:21-31, we encounter in a compressed form Paul's explanation of the way God's righteousness is effective in and through Christ's atonement to bring justification to sinners who believe. In this paragraph words of the *dikaio*-stem occur nine times while there are another nine occurrences of words for *faith* and *believing*. Chapter 4 provides the important illustration of Abraham, who was justified not by his obedience to God but by his faith and trust in God. At this point the argument of Paul is similar to that found in the letter to Galatia.

The contents of the next three chapters (5—8) may be seen as an explanation of what justification by faith means and entails. There is freedom from death, sin and the Law with new life in the Spirit of Christ. Again we note links with the contents of the letter to Galatia. Having received God's righteousness by faith, the believer is delivered from eternal death and the wrath to come (5:9) and will be given salvation at the Last Judgment. Here and now he experiences a freedom from the power of sin and he is enabled to live according to God's will (6:16). The old Law of Moses is no longer a threat to him; he now lives in the power of the indwelling Spirit, who brings the love of God to his heart and assures him he is a child of God (8:15, 16). Chapters 9—11 have sometimes been seen as a digression from the main theme. It is far better, however, to see their contents as a whole and to view Paul wrestling with the problem of the history and destiny of the Jews in the light of the revelation of God's righteousness in the gospel. Finally, while it is true that *dikaio*-stem words are rare in chapters 12— 15, the material in them is about the obedience to God of those who have been declared righteous before God. In fact, without the previous teaching on justification these final chapters would have no base for the obedience they describe.

Having given an overall sketch of the theme of righteousness/ justification in the letter, it is now appropriate to examine in a little more detail particular parts.

1:16, 17

> I am not ashamed of the gospel, because it is the power of God for the salvation of everyone who believes: first for the Jew, then for the Gentile. For in the gospel a righteousness from God is revealed, a righteousness that is by faith from first to last, just as it is written: "The righteous will live by faith."

This good news is for the whole world—"everyone." And because it is the effectual word of the Lord proclaimed in the power of the Holy Spirit, it achieves results; it brings salvation to sinners, Jew and Gentile, who receive and believe it. The clue to the saving power of the gospel of God lies in the fact that God has acted in righteousness to make provision in Christ for human salvation. This means that God now reckons as righteous in his sight those who believe. The "righteousness of God" (KJV) is best understood (as is apparently the case in the NIV) as a genitive of authorship meaning, "the righteousness which goes forth from God." Luther, however, took it to be an objective genitive meaning, "the righteousness which is valid before God." The function of the quotation from the prophet Habakkuk is to emphasize faith as

the only right response to God, the righteous Lord.
3:21-26

> But now a righteousness from God, apart from law, has been
> made known, to which the Law and the Prophets testify. This
> righteousness from God comes through faith in Jesus Christ to all
> who believe. There is no difference, for all have sinned and fall
> short of the glory of God, and are justified freely by his grace
> through the redemption that came by Christ Jesus. God present-
> ed him as a sacrifice of atonement, through faith in his blood. He
> did this to demonstrate his justice, because in his forbearance he
> had left the sins committed beforehand unpunished—he did it to
> demonstrate his justice at the present time, so as to be just and the
> one who justifies the man who has faith in Jesus.

It is possible that Paul adapted here a Jewish-Christian formula, but of
this we cannot be sure and must understand it in its Pauline form. In
verse 21 the "now" refers to the special period of time (eschatological)
between the exaltation of the Messiah and his return in glory as judge;
"law" in that verse is probably shorthand for "the demands imposed by
a collection of commandments." The righteousness of God is revealed
and set forth in the achievement of Jesus as Messiah and in the proclamation of the gospel of God concerning him. Though this righteousness has nothing to do with law, the contents of the books of Moses and
of the prophets of Israel testify to it. This righteousness (v. 22) is
available from God to all who believe the good news concerning Jesus,
the Messiah. In fact (v. 23), everyone needs this gift of righteousness,
for all human beings are declared by God to be sinners. As the judge of
the world, God freely declares sinners to be righteous on the basis of
the liberation Jesus the Messiah achieved for mankind through his
death and resurrection (v. 24). Jesus died at Calvary as a sacrifice for sin
(v. 25) so that God could declare sinners righteous on the basis of his
perfect atonement for sin. Sinners have to do nothing but accept the
gift by faith.
    Verses 25b and 26 are difficult to understand. The NIV uses the
noun "justice" twice in preference to "righteousness," which is used in
verses 21 and 22. Other translations (RSV, TEV) keep to the one word
"righteousness" throughout this section. The meaning appears to be
that the death of Christ, as a divine act of righteousness, proved that
God is righteous yet merciful. For in the act of demonstrating that he is
a just/righteous God, he provides also the means by which the believer
can be put into a right relationship with himself and forgives sins.
Before the atonement of Christ, God had passed over past sins but had
not forgiven them. Now because the death of Christ is a righteous and
saving act of God, sins can truly be forgiven. It is probable that Paul
had in mind that Christ's "sacrifice of atonement" (v. 25) averted the
wrath of God and functioned as a propitiatory as well as expiatory

sacrifice; the Greek *hilastērion* certainly suggests this.

What comes out clearly in this section is that God's activity in restoring sinners to a right relationship with himself is centered on the cross; thus justification cannot be separated from the "his blood" and "a sacrifice of atonement" by Christ. In the language of later theology, the sacrificial death of Christ is the meritorious cause of our justification.

6:19

> RSV: For just as you once yielded your members to impurity and to greater and greater iniquity, so now yield your members to righteousness for sanctification.

> NIV: Just as you used to offer the parts of your body in slavery to impurity and to ever-increasing wickedness, so now offer them in slavery to righteousness and holiness.

> TEV: At one time you surrendered yourselves entirely as slaves to impurity and wickedness, for wicked purposes. In the same way you must surrender yourselves entirely as slaves of righteousness, for holy purposes.

Here Paul is contrasting two ways of life, the pagan and the Christian. In 6:15-19, what is made clear is that those who submit to the gospel of God by believing are actually by such faith also committing themselves to obedience to God's will and a new way of life. True faith is faith-obedience (or faith that is faithful). In verse 19 a believer is described as a slave of righteousness (= God acting in righteousness) for a life of consecration/holiness. (The basic idea of holiness is, being set apart for God and his service.) This verse or section does not endorse the idea that a person is first justified/declared righteous and then (later or gradually) sanctified. Rather, the idea is that being in a right relationship with God as judge and heavenly Father, the believer is thereby consecrated to the service of the Lord. Justification and consecration belong together. Not a little harm has been done by those preachers who have rigidly imposed upon Paul's teaching a division between justification (understood as what God declares in Heaven) and sanctification (understood as what God does in us here on earth). It is not quite so simple, for as we shall see in Chapter 4 of this book, justification and sanctification are two complementary ways of describing the gracious activity of God.

10:3, 4

> NIV: Since they disregarded the righteousness that comes from God and sought to establish their own, they did not submit to God's righteousness. Christ is the end of the law so that there may be righteousness for everyone who believes.

TEV: They have not known the way in which God puts people
right with himself, and have tried to set up their own way:
and so they did not submit themselves to God's way of
putting people right. For Christ has brought the Law to an
end, so that everyone who believes is put right with God.

In this part of the letter Paul is relating the righteousness of God to the
history and destiny of the Jewish people, and he is also contrasting
justification by faith and justification by works. Pious Jews were not
aware that in the gospel God himself has revealed a righteousness
which is a gift accompanying a right relationship with himself. They
have sought to achieve by their works their own type of righteousness,
hoping that this would be acceptable and place them in a right relationship with God. They have not allowed themselves to be placed (by
faith) in the presence of God, the judge, so that he could declare them
righteous in his sight through Christ. For the truth is that Christ has
put an end to the use of the Law of Moses as the basis for righteous
status before God through doing the deeds of the Law. The battle is
faith versus works, and God has already decided in favor of faith. This
fact is made abundantly clear in verses 5-13.

These four extracts from the letter have served to make clear four
aspects of Paul's doctrine of justification by faith. It is all about the
righteousness which goes forth from God to be the power within his
gospel; it is inseparably bound to the "sacrifice of atonement" offered
by Christ; it has a built-in requirement of consecration of life to God's
service; and it stands opposed to all schemes which allow for human
achievement in gaining a righteous status before the Lord.

To say the least, justification is a dominant perspective in Paul's
theology. To say the most, it is its central theme. Certainly Luther
believed that it was the central theme of Paul's teaching concerning the
gospel of God, and he has been followed by many Protestant theologians in this evaluation. Perhaps there is not one truly dominant theme
in Paul's writings but a cluster of prominent themes (e.g., reconciliation, salvation-history, justification and "in Christ"). It is best to view
these major themes as related to each other in terms of a cluster of
different but complementary models or metaphors, each of which highlights an important aspect of the work of God in Christ for and in us.
To try to arrange the different major and minor themes in Paul in an
ordo salutis (order of salvation) is to misunderstand their function.
They overlap in meaning and cannot be put into a logical order. We
shall perhaps become more aware of this as we note below how sanctification is used in Paul's letters and other parts of the New Testament.
Here the point may be illustrated with reference to forgiveness and
adoption, minor themes in Paul's writings.

The verb *aphiēmi,* meaning "to forgive," occurs forty-five times in
the New Testament, of which only one is in Paul's letters (Romans 4:7).

The noun *aphesis* ("forgiveness") is found only in Ephesians 1:7 and Colossians 1:14. The related word *paresis*, meaning "letting go unpunished," occurs only in Romans 3:25. These three or four instances indicate that forgiveness is a minor theme. And it remains a minor theme if we add the occasions when the verb *charizomai* (= to be gracious to) occurs with a sense near to the idea of *aphiēmi*—see 2 Corinthians 2:7, 10; 12:13; Ephesians 4:32; Colossians 2:13; 3:13. Forgiveness includes both making of no account the sin that has been committed and the acceptance of the sinner, be it between God and man or between man and man. Since Paul makes much use of the two great themes of justification and reconciliation, he has little need to use that of forgiveness. There is an overlap of meaning between forgiveness and justification as well as between forgiveness and reconciliation.

The legal word *huiothesia*, which describes the "making" or "adopting" of a son, is used of what God the Father does to Christians (Rom. 8:15, 23; Gal. 4:5; Eph. 1:5), as well as to ancient Israel (Rom. 9:4). The contexts in which the word occurs shows that it has reference to the present in anticipation of the future and that it is closely connected with the gift of the indwelling Spirit. The Holy Spirit testifies to the human spirit that adoption has taken place, but believers still "wait eagerly for our adoption as sons, the redemption of our bodies" (Rom. 8:15-23). So it is not a simple story—as in some popular accounts of Paul's theology—of justification being followed in an *ordo salutis* by adoption. The relation of the theme of justification to that of adoption cannot be forced into any chronological or logical order, for they are complementary metaphors and models.

Not only must we hesitate to turn Paul's complementary metaphors into descriptions of parts of a process that has logical or chronological sequence; we must also be cautious in taking metaphors from others parts of the New Testament (e.g., regeneration from the Johannine documents) and making them fit into a scheme whose major parts come from Paul. While there is a profound and deep unity in the teaching of the New Testament, there is also a diversity which must be respected. The teaching on justification in Paul's letters is a distinct and powerful example of the diversity of ways in which the New Testament explains the power of the gospel.

3   FAITH ACCORDING TO JAMES

A truth presented in two dissimilar situations easily appears to be two different truths. Our natural inclination when we speak to people is to accommodate or tailor what we have to say so that they can, from within their situation, appreciate the message. For example, suppose my message is: "For the good of the country, the government requires all people of eighteen years to do military service for one year." The way I present the need and importance of this military service will differ, perhaps greatly, in my address to a club of retired army officers and in my chat to teenagers at a youth club. Further, if two people are involved in communicating this message and if each one goes to a separate group, then the differences between the two presentations will be obvious.

The clue to the different presentations of the combined theme of justification-works-faith in the letters of Paul and the letter of James is that each writer was addressing a separate problem from a distinct perspective. Both were in agreement that the gospel of God calls for and creates saving faith in us; further, both held that such genuine faith should be expressed in a new quality of life. Yet each had his own ministry in a particular context with specific needs and questions. Therefore, in presenting the one truth in these two very different human and religious situations, it is not surprising that the emphasis of each one is not identical. James is the leader of the Christian community in Jerusalem and writes for Christian Jews.[1] Paul is the apostle to the Gentiles and writes to the churches he has founded or with which he wants to make contact. It should not surprise us that we have to make an effort to recognize the unity within the dissimiliarity.

Martin Luther was unable to see this unity. He referred to James' letter as "an epistle of straw" and dismissed its teaching as "contradicting St. Paul and the rest of Scripture by giving righteousness to works."

Like others of his day, he believed the letter should not have been included in the canon of the New Testament. Happily today, both from a scholarly perspective and the needs of ministry at the grassroots level, we can perceive the need for the teaching of both St. Paul and St. James. The actual tension they set up in our thinking is the very tension we find in seeking to live as Christians today.

The passage in James which is the center of discussion is 2:14-26, which may be entitled, "Christian Faith Expressed in Christian Deeds."

> What good is it, my brothers, if a man claims to have faith but has no deeds? Can such faith save him? Suppose a brother or sister is without clothes and daily food. If one of you says to him, "Go, I wish you well; keep warm and well fed," but does nothing about his physical needs, what good is it? In the same way, faith by itself, if it is not accompanied by action, is dead. (vv. 14-17)

Where the NIV translates the Greek *ergon* as "deeds" the RSV has "works" and the TEV "actions." Paul taught that salvation is by faith and not by deeds/works/actions. James teaches that faith must be accompanied by deeds/works/actions. Why? Paul had in mind those actions done to fulfill the requirements of the Law of Moses so one can claim that the Law has been obeyed. James has in mind here deeds or actions of love. These may be understood as all types of duties, inward and outward—thoughts as well as words and actions (towards God or to human beings) which proceed from a heart and will that love God and seek to please him. James saw very clearly that genuine faith is inevitably linked to authentic works of love, especially within the Church, the community of love.

James proceeded to face the challenge of those who said: "I have faith; I know and accept the Christian creed. However, I cannot see that Christian behavior is absolutely required by the Christian creed. Surely it is enough merely to believe." If James wrote before Paul, then here we have an example of a particular heresy which arose in early Jewish Christianity. If he wrote after Paul's teaching on justification by faith was known, then he was facing an exaggerated (and therefore unfair) presentation of Pauline theology.

> But someone will say, "You have faith; I have deeds." Show me your faith without deeds, and I will show you my faith by what I do. You believe that there is one God. Good! Even the demons believe that—and shudder. (vv. 18, 19)

There are several problems of translation here (as a comparison of the English versions reveals). What James is saying is something like this: "You who are in error claim to have faith, and I make the claim by God's grace to have works and deeds. I can prove the existence of my faith as well as its quality by my actions and behavior. But I challenge you, indeed I defy you, to prove to me or any rational being either the existence or the quality of your faith. It is my conviction that without Christian action and behavior you cannot possibly have genuine faith in your hearts." The proof of the pudding, as we say, is in the eating, and the proof that anyone truly believes and trusts in God is that he lives in a manner which is pleasing to God. Faith is not only a matter of believing that God exists and that Jesus is the Messiah; it is also a matter of trusting God and obeying him. If faith were only a matter of believing that God and Christ exist, the devils would be justified and saved!

It was impossible for anyone to discuss the topic of faith and deeds/works without making reference to Abraham because of his unique place in the covenant God made with his people. Still addressing the person whom he judged to be in error, James continues in verses 20-24:

> You foolish man, do you want evidence that faith without deeds is useless? Was not our ancestor Abraham considered righteous for what he did when he offered his son Isaac on the altar? You see that his faith and his actions were working together, and his faith was made complete by what he did. And the scripture was fulfilled that says, "Abraham believed God, and it was credited to him as righteousness," and he was called God's friend. You see that a person is justified by what he does and not by faith alone.

The readiness of Abraham to sacrifice Isaac was the greatest trial of his faith—as Genesis 22 makes clear. His unquestioning and simple faith in God revealed a trust in the Lord like that a child has in his parent—as Hebrews 11:17-19 celebrates. His readiness to sacrifice was a deed of love for God which showed that he was in a right relationship with God—he was considered righteous. This and other deeds of love were the products of real faith, a faith that came to maturity (completion) in Abraham's acts of obedience to God's call and direction. In fact, the sacrifice of Isaac as a deed of love is to be interpreted as a fulfillment of Abraham's justification by faith (Gen. 15:6).

It is to be noted that where Paul employs the example of Abraham to dismiss the claim of salvation by works of the Law of Moses, James uses it to illustrate the futility of a dead faith. James saw Abraham as a man with genuine and living faith which had to find expression in deeds of love. In his way of understanding the matter, Genesis 15:6 is to be interpreted by Genesis 22: faith and works of love are necessary for justification—a right relationship with God. In contrast, Paul talked of faith alone and the fruit of righteousness (Phil. 1:11). Both Paul and James saw an integral connection between the Christian creed and the Christian ethic. Faith alone justifies, but the faith that justifies is not alone.

forensic: suitable for public debate (like that used in a court of law)

The final part of 2:14-26 presents Rahab as an unexpected example of justification by faith and works of love.

> In the same way, was not even Rahab the prostitute considered righteous for what she did when she gave lodging to the spies and sent them off in a different direction? As the body without the spirit is dead, so faith without deeds is dead. (vv. 25, 26)

Rahab was a Canaanite woman who had been a prostitute and who became a proselyte, and thereby a member of Israel (Josh. 2). By her conduct in helping the men of Israel, she offered proof that real faith expresses itself in deeds of love. Thus through the example of patriarch and prostitute James sought to prove that justification is by a true faith which operates in, cooperates with, and is vindicated by works. Faith without deeds of love is not a genuine faith: it is that kind of believing of which demons are capable.

The difference of emphasis between Paul and James may be expressed in terms of the Old Testament theme of ṣdq, which we noted has both a forensic and an ethical import. It is clear that in Paul's teaching the forensic idea of righteousness (being declared righteous by God the judge) is prominent. In contrast, for James there is the dual emphasis of righteousness/justification as both acceptance in God's sight and as deeds of love. Rightly to understand Paul is to accept the teaching of James since Paul looked to all who are justified by faith to be those in whose lives the fruit of the Spirit could be seen.

We have noted how Martin Luther failed to grasp the particular message of James. He tended to assume that the "works" or "deeds" were identical in the teaching of the two apostles. Before Luther's time the most influential attempt to overcome the apparent contradictions in the two writers came from Augustine of Hippo (to whose teaching on justification we turn in Part 2). He claimed that Paul referred to "works" that preceded faith while James referred to "works" which followed faith. This solution is true of James but not of Paul. As we saw, Paul was against "works" which were offered to God to gain justification, whether before faith or after it. The other major point that Augustine made was to distinguish between "dead faith" which even the devils possess (Jas. 2:19) and the true faith which is both active in love (Gal. 5:6) and revealed in "works" (Jas. 2:18).

If we think of the different theologies (Pauline, Johannine, Lukan, etc.) of the New Testament along the analogy of the rainbow (which is a unity of seven colors—red to violet), then we can say that while they certainly belong together in the one Testament, the theologies of Paul and James on justification are as different as the two most dissimilar colors in the rainbow. However, as we need those two very different colors to have a rainbow, so we need the differing emphases of James and Paul in the Bible and in the Church.

4 THE HOLINESS OF THE SAINTS

"Holy" and "holiness" are words often used in the vocabulary of worship and prayer. Catholic Christians talk about the "holiness" of the "saints," and Protestant Christians sometimes speak of the need for "sanctification" in their lives. All types of Christians pray, "Our Father who art in heaven, hallowed be thy name." In the Greek New Testament, "holy" translates *hagios* (*hagiotēs* is "holiness"; *hagioi* are "saints"; and *hagiazō* is "to sanctify" or "to hallow"). In the Latin New Testament the equivalent words are *sanctus, sanctitas, sancti* and *sanctifico*. So while the Greek of the New Testament uses one basic word, *hagios*, and its cognates, the English we speak uses words from Old English (*halig,* holy) and the Latin, (*sanctus*) to translate it. Thus the relation of "holiness" and "sanctification" is much the same as that we noted between "righteousness" and "justification."

In the English New Testament, "holy" is commonly used to translate the Greek *hagios*, "holiness" *(hagiotes)*, and "saints" *(hagioi)*. So we shall look first at holiness and sanctification in the Old Testament and then turn to the New Testament. We shall find out that there is not one simple meaning but a cluster of related meanings.

The Old Testament[1]

Wherever God's presence was felt, the Israelites encountered the wonder and mystery of holiness. Take the events recorded in Exodus 19 as an example. The people of Israel, recently liberated from Egypt, were camped near Mount Sinai. Moses went up the mountain to hear from the Lord, who was about to make a covenant (agreement) with this people. The way in which God revealed himself on the mountain and his call for consecration from the people illustrate the wonder and mystery of holiness.

God revealed himself as the holy Lord: "Mount Sinai was covered with smoke, because the LORD descended on it in fire. The smoke billowed up from it like smoke from a furnace, the whole mountain trembled violently, and the sound of the trumpet grew louder and louder" (vv. 18, 19). The association of holiness and fire is common in the Old Testament (see also 2 Sam. 22:9ff.; Ezek. 1:4ff.); and in the New Testament God is described as "a consuming fire" (Heb. 12:26-29). A great fire attracts by its powerful light and repels by its heat, and these two characteristics well represent the holiness of God.

The people sanctified themselves by washing their clothing, by abstaining from sexual relations and by not touching the mountain where the theophany (= temporal and spatial manifestation of God) took place. Sanctification, or the act of making holy, is the transition from the realm of the profane to that of direct association with God. In this case the people were responding to the call of God, who had liberated them from the slavery of Egypt and was about to renew (in a special form of administration) the covenant of grace he had made with their ancestor, Abraham. They were to be "a kingdom of priests and a holy nation" (19:6). Within the covenant (Ex. 20ff.), they learned that not only as a total people were they holy (that is, set apart for God), but that there was also a santification of certain times, space, things and persons. They were to keep holy the Sabbath day (Ex. 20:8) and the festivals (Lev. 23:4ff.). The land in which they were to live was God's territory, and so must not be polluted with idolatry and immorality; it was holy ground (Lev. 18:27, 28). Jerusalem was to become the holy city (Isa. 8:18; 18:7; 30:29). Especially holy was the Tabernacle (and then the Temple), along with its furniture and vessels (Ex. 30:25-29; 40:9-11; Lev. 8:10ff.). Finally the persons of the ministers of the sanctuary were holy (Ex. 30:30; 40:13ff.). Thus, by his call and covenant the Lord made his people holy; but they expressed this sanctification in terms of making themselves holy in the ways God directed. They thereby showed that they belonged to the holy Lord and were not as other nations.

The revelation of the Lord on Mount Sinai emphasized the unapproachableness and remoteness of the Lord. Whoever stared at the holy mountain when the Lord descended perished (Ex. 19:21; cf. Judg. 13:22), for no person may see God and live (Ex. 33:20). This aspect of the holiness of God is particularly evident in the terrifying stories of the impact of the holy ark of the covenant upon the men of Beth Shemesh (1 Sam. 6:19, 20) and the Philistines (2 Sam. 6, 7). The ark was holy because it served as the symbol of the holy Lord's covenant with a holy nation. To examine it out of curiosity was to trifle with the holy Lord— just as touching or looking at the mountain at the time of the theophany was to trifle with his holiness. We read, "God struck down some of the men of Beth Shemesh, putting seventy of them to death because they had looked into the ark of the LORD. The people mourned because of the heavy blow the LORD had dealt them, and the men of Beth Shemesh asked, 'Who can stand in the presence of the LORD, this holy God? To whom will the ark go up from here?' " (1 Sam. 6:19, 20). There is a distance between the Lord and human beings which is more than the distinction between eternity/infinity and space/time.

Perhaps the most well-known presentation of God as holy in the Old Testament is that found in Isaiah 6, the vision of the prophet. He saw the Lord exalted above the Temple but nevertheless filling the Temple with his glorious robe. The seraphim, as servants of the Lord, called one to another, "Holy, holy, holy is the LORD Almighty; the whole earth is full of his glory." God's holiness as encountered by Isaiah was not only his wholly otherness; it was also his total perfection and absolute purity. He is separated from the creation, though his glory fills it; he is also separated from all impurity and sin, though he will cleanse it. Isaiah had to confess, "Woe to me! I am ruined! For I am a man of unclean lips, and I live among a people of unclean lips, and my eyes have seen the King, the LORD Almighty." God, the Holy One, commanded one of the seraphs to minister to Isaiah and with a coal from the burning sacrifice of atonement to touch his lips and cleanse him from sin. Thus cleansed, he was able to respond to the call of God to go as the divine messenger to the people of Israel.

It is clear that the holiness of God in the experience and teaching of Isaiah includes an ethical dimension of moral purity. But it would be false (as in some popular Christian thinking) to reduce the holiness of God to moral categories alone. The transcendence, apartness and otherness of God remain when the moral attributes have been exhausted. In fact, God acts in righteousness to save and to punish because he is first and foremost holy. Isaiah recognized this: "But the LORD Almighty will be exalted by his justice, and the holy God will show himself holy by his righteousness" (5:16). Further, Isaiah taught that God makes himself known as the Holy One who in his holiness redeems his people (41:14; 43:4, 14; 47:4; 49:7; 54:5) and executes judgment (1:4-9; 5:13-16; 30:8-14).

The definite association of holiness with love/mercy in God reaches its clearest portrayal in the Old Testament in the book of Hosea. Through his experience as a husband of an unfaithful wife, this prophet learned about God's holy hatred of sin and his love for sinners. The apparent tension between holiness (which must destroy sin) and mercy (which works for the restoration of sinners) is conveyed in some of Hosea's prophetic oracles. For example, the Lord spoke to him about both what he, the Lord, ought to do and what he would do for his people who had betrayed and forsaken him: "I will not carry out my fierce anger, nor devastate Ephraim again. For I am God, and not man—the Holy One among you. I will not come in wrath" (11:9). Later the Lord said, "I will heal their waywardness and love them freely, for my anger has turned away from them" (14:4). Hosea learned that the Lord is holy *and* merciful. But for a full picture of God's holy love we have to read the New Testament.

The holiness of God cannot be presented merely as his wholly otherness, but must also be expressed in terms of eternal moral perfection; likewise the holiness of God's people cannot merely be seen in terms of separation from wickedness, but must also be seen in terms of a morally upright life. Leviticus 19 provides an excellent example of this principle. Moses was commanded by the Lord: "Speak to the entire assembly of Israel and say to them: 'Be holy because I, the LORD your God, am holy.' " Then follows a long list of commandments in the keeping of which as God's separated people they will express holiness in terms of moral integrity. These commandments refer both to external behavior (e.g., not to defraud the neighbor) and to right attitudes (e.g., not to hate the brother but to love the neighbor as oneself). Holiness in Israel included righteousness of life in thought, word and deed. Further, as Psalm 15 clearly indicates, only "he whose walk is blameless and who does what is righteous" is to live on the holy hill of Zion and worship the Lord, the Holy One. God's setting us apart as his people should lead to a reflection in daily life of his moral purity and perfection.

The New Testament[2]
The writers of the New Testament assume that God is holy. Only seldom, however, do they explicitly say so (e.g., Rev. 4:6-10; 16:4-7; 1 Pet. 1:15, 16; John 17:11). On a few occasions Jesus is called holy (e.g., Luke 1:35; Mark 1:24; John 6:69; Acts 3:14; 4:30; Rev. 3:7). Further, in the style of the Old Testament, things and places are sometimes called holy—e.g., the "Holy Scriptures" (Rom. 1:2) and the "holy" law of God (Rom. 7:12). Perhaps the best way to state the difference between the Old and New Testaments is to say that in the New there is a great emphasis on the presence and work of the Spirit of God as *Holy* Spirit. As the One who bears the name and characteristics of Jesus (John 14—16), the Holy Spirit as the Paraclete sets people apart for God in the name of Jesus, the Holy One and Messiah. They can be set apart for God because of the sacrificial blood of Jesus, shed for the remission of their sins (Heb. 10:29). We are set apart for God by the atoning work of Christ, and we are set apart for God in the work of the Holy Spirit. The one is done once and for all; the other is done continually in the Church on earth until the end of the age. Sanctification, like justification, is clearly the work of God.

The teaching of the Apostle Paul concerning sanctification may be said to begin with the idea that believers are presented to God the Father in Jesus Christ, who is their holiness/sanctification. In Christ we were chosen by God out of all peoples and placed on God's side in Christ and dedicated to his service. "You are in Christ Jesus, who has become for us wisdom from God—that is, our righteousness, holiness and redemption" (1 Cor. 1:30). Only in Christ do we have a right relationship with God ("Christ . . . our righteousness") and a place by God's side over against the profane world ("Christ . . . our holiness"). The Church is composed of those who are "sanctified in Christ Jesus"

(1 Cor. 1:2). Put another way, the community of believers is "called to be saints" (Rom. 1:7), so that local churches may be described as "the congregations of the saints" (1 Cor. 14:33). In Christ all believers are saints. Martyrdom or great personal virtue is not a prerequisite because, as Paul told the church in Corinth, "You were washed, you were sanctified, you were justified in the name of the Lord Jesus Christ and by the Spirit of our God" (1 Cor. 6:11). The church is the community of the sanctified and the congregation of the saints.

The people who are already made holy in Christ are called to be holy in daily living. "It is God's will that you should be holy; that you should avoid sexual immorality; that each of you should learn to control his own body in a way that is holy and honorable, not in passionate lust like the heathen, who do not know God" (1 Thess. 4:3-5). For Paul it is crystal-clear that "God did not call us to be impure, but to live a holy life" (1 Thess. 4:7). In looking at the apostle's teaching on righteousness and holiness in Romans 6:19-22, we noted in Chapter 2 that sanctification has reference to that segment of the Christian life which involves total dedication to the service of the holy Lord.

Since the concept of holiness is much used in the Old Testament with reference to the cultus—the place and means of the worship of God the Holy One—it is not surprising that Paul uses this association to emphasize both the consecration to God and the purity of life required by those who are consecrated to such a deity. The Church is a holy temple (1 Cor. 3:16, 17; Eph. 2:21); believers are to present their bodies to God in the form of living, holy sacrifices (Rom. 12:1). In fact, Christ sanctified the whole Church and made it his own by his sacrifice at Calvary, so he could present it as a pure, spotless sacrifice at the end of the age (Eph 5:27).

Holiness, a state of belonging to God and being dedicated to him, relates directly to the Church's being called to service and sacrifice in the power of the Holy Spirit. It will not surprise us that whenever Paul used the verb *hagiazō* the subject was always God the Father, Jesus Christ or the Holy Spirit. *Sanctification is the work of God.* However, Paul did sometimes use the noun sanctification *(hagiasmos)* in such a manner as to suggest that for the actual realization of sanctification in the life of the Church and its individual members, the total commitment and dedication of the believers is required (2 Tim. 2:15; 1 Thess. 4:7). But in the strict sense there is no such thing as self-sanctification. It is a work of God into which he nevertheless calls for and makes use of the cooperation of the whole Christian community.

In the letter to the Hebrews (which in the history of the Church has often been regarded as written by Paul) Christ is presented as the sanctifier of his people. "We have been made holy through the sacrifice of the body of Jesus Christ once for all" (10:10). Here the perfect tense of *hagiazō* is used, conveying the idea of something done once for all time. By the sacrificial death of Jesus we have been placed on God's side and consecrated to him forever. At 10:14 there is a change of tense:

"By one sacrifice he has made perfect forever those who are being made holy." Here the verb "perfect" is in the perfect tense, referring to that perfection of the people of God which is accomplished once and for all by Christ our High Priest in his mediatorial work. In 10:29 we read of "the blood of the covenant that sanctified" the Christians; this refers to Christ's inaugurating the new covenant by his sacrificial death and thus setting the people of the new covenant on God's side. We also read at 13:12, "Jesus also suffered outside the city gate to make the people holy through his own blood." This is a reference to Golgotha, situated outside the city walls of old Jerusalem where Jesus suffered in order to sanctify his people and to bring them to God. Because Christ is our sanctifier, let us "through Jesus Christ . . . continually offer to God a sacrifice of praise—the fruit of lips that confess his name. And do not forget to do good and to share with others, for with such sacrifices God is pleased" (13:15, 16). Here the association of worship and holiness is clear; the holy sanctuary of the old covenant becomes the holy people of the new covenant.

Finally we need to notice the use of the great Old Testament call to holiness among God's people as cited by the Apostle Peter: "As obedient children, do not conform to the evil desires you had when you lived in ignorance. But just as he who called you is holy, so be holy in all you do; for it is written: 'Be holy, because I am holy'" (1 Pet. 1:14-16). Here the ethical dimension is prominent. Christians are to show their consecration to God by the way they live.

Justification and Sanctification Compared[3]

If we examine the relationship of justification and sanctification in the letters of Paul (or in the whole of the New Testament) we cannot simply conclude that we are first declared righteous and then made holy by God—justification followed by sanctification. The relationship is more subtle. First of all, the words gain their meaning from different contexts; justification is a forensic term, while sanctification is a cultic metaphor. Thus their meanings can often be parallel without being identical—sanctified in Christ and justified in Christ. Here the tense is past tense, for in the death and resurrection of Christ the people of God are already justified and sanctified. The one has reference to being declared in a right relationship with God the Father; the other has reference to being placed on God's side and consecrated to his service.

In the second place, while justification has a primary reference to God's personal relationship (as judge) with the individual believer, declaring him to be in the right, sanctification normally describes what God does for his people and calls for from them as a whole—"called to be saints" and made a "holy nation." Certainly at a secondary level of meaning, to be justified also means being placed with others in the covenant of grace; and to be sanctified must have personal reference as well as a community dimension, for a community is composed of persons.

Thirdly, justification as an act of God, the judge, has no explicit reference to the actual making of a person righteous in a moral sense. An implicit reference, however, is there since it is the one Lord who pronounces acquittal and calls for right relationships with the Church and the world. In contrast, sanctification often has an explicit reference to actually making the Christian community holy in terms of moral perfection. Thus, the idea of sanctification has a larger reference than justification, for it describes what the people of God are in Christ and what they are to become in real-life situations. Thus in sanctification, understood as that which takes place on earth under the control of the *Holy* Spirit, God calls for the wholehearted response and self-dedication of believers. In justification there is only one appropriate response to God's Word and promise, and that is believing submission to the Word of the living God.

God's justification of the sinner must lead to ethical, internal sanctification; but justification can never be based on man's ethical attainments. God's justification must lead to righteousness of life, but such righteousness of life is never the basis for God's justification. The only ground for our justification before God is what the Lord Jesus Christ has done for us in death and resurrection; he, and he alone, is our righteousness. Likewise, the only basis of our sanctification before God and within us is the saving work of Christ, who is our holiness. Our sanctification in Christ before God must lead to a righteous life, but right deeds and right relationships can never be used for our sanctification before the Father. It is clear that the only source of our justification and sanctification is God—Father, Son and Holy Spirit.

When we come to study Protestant theology in Part 2, we shall see that sanctification has often been understood solely in terms of a process within the Church and the believer of a growth towards perfection in love. Its reference to our objective standing as already sanctified before the Father has been little emphasized in dogmatic theology. Another related matter is also worth mentioning here. In Protestant systematic theology the concept of regeneration or new birth by the Spirit has often been presented as the beginning of the process of sanctification—the idea being that new birth begins new life. It is not necessary to supply here a sketch of the New Testament teaching on regeneration. It is perhaps sufficient to remark that the word or its cognates is rarely used by Paul (see Titus 3:5 though), who apparently preferred the alternative picture of "new creation" (see 2 Cor. 5:17). However, in the Johannine material the picture of new birth (or birth from God who is above) comes fairly often (see John 1:13; 3:3, 7; 1 John 2:29; 3:9; 4:7). The New Testament use of *regeneration* implies more than the beginning of a process. Its full meaning may be said to overlap at certain points with the meaning of sanctification (when understood as the process moving towards moral perfection). Regeneration and sanctification cannot merely be seen in the New Testament as the beginning and continuation of a process. There is much, much more to the dynamic of life in Christ than this.

Part 2: Historical

5 Augustine and Aquinas

Writing in 1874, the Scottish theologian Robert Rainy claimed that the tenet of justification by faith was the result of a genuine doctrinal development.[1] As dogma, justification through the imputed righteousness of Christ and by faith had not been explicitly taught in the post-apostolic, pre-Luther Church. This claim may come as a surprise to some Protestants, for it has been common to assert that the doctrine of Luther was the recovery of the doctrine taught by Augustine of Hippo or by one or other of the late medieval theologians.

For example, G. S. Faber, an Anglican clergyman, authored *The Primitive Doctrine of Justification* (1837) in which he claimed that the teaching of Protestantism was in substance the same as that of the early Greek and Latin fathers of the Church. James Buchanan, a Free Church of Scotland clergyman, wrote a major book, *The Doctrine of Justification* (1867) in which he confidently appealed to the patristic period. He wrote:

> It is of special importance that the precise object and reason of any appeal to the Fathers on the subject of justification should be distinctly understood. It is simply to prove a matter of FACT, in opposition to an erroneous assertion—the fact, namely, that the Protestant doctrine of justification was not a novelty introduced for the first time by Luther and Calvin—that it was held and taught, more or less explicitly, by some writers in every successive age—and that there is no truth in the allegation that it had been unknown for 1,400 years before the Reformation. (p. 94)

A careful study of the quotations supplied by Faber and Buchanan proves only one thing—the early Fathers believed that salvation is by grace. The Victorians claimed too much and read back into an earlier period the structure of thought which belonged to a later period. This will become apparent as we look at the teaching of Augustine and Aquinas.

"Deification"

To look for serious discussions on justification in the writings of the Fathers before Augustine is to look in vain. Apparently no theologian or biblical commentator felt a need to attempt to translate St. Paul's teaching on righteousness and faith into contemporary terms. This may be accounted for in terms of a decline in the doctrine of grace. More probably it was because it was held that Paul's teaching had a particular reference to the problem of Judaizers in the Church, and this problem had long since departed. Whatever the reason, the Christian life was not seen in terms of justification. If there was a dominant way of looking at the Christian life, it was in terms of what was then called "deification," giving the word a different meaning than that which we so quickly attribute to it today.

The idea of deification or divinization as taught in the patristic period has often been misunderstood by Protestants.[2] It has been seen as contrary to Scripture, as blurring the distinction between God and man, and as distinctively "Eastern" in tone and content. It is found in the teaching of both Eastern and Western fathers up to Augustine (and afterwards). However, it is more usual today to think of it as an Eastern or Orthodox (Greek and Russian) doctrine.[3]

When the teachers of the early Church spoke of deification or divinization, there was no intention of claiming consubstantiality with God, for, in the words of the Creed, only Christ is one in substance with the Father. The idea could rather be summarized something like this: the eternal Logos became flesh and dwelt among us in order to live our life, face our temptations, die for us and be exalted for us; as the second Adam and thus as representative man, what he did as One who possessed our human nature he actually did for all of us—especially those of the human race who by the Holy Spirit are in union with him. Salvation is wrought by Christ for us and is achieved in us when his Spirit dwells in our hearts. The biblical basis of such teaching was anchored firmly in the Word-flesh Christology of John's Gospel.

Further, man was seen in terms of the description in Genesis— made "in the image and likeness of God." The image had been impaired and the likeness defaced through sin and Satan, but grace would renew and renovate every believing individual after the pattern of Christ, the true image of God. St. Paul's teaching concerning becoming sons of God by adoption and possessing the Spirit as the seal of sonship (Rom. 8) was also important—even more so perhaps than the famous statement of 2 Peter 1:4 that Christians are "partakers of the divine nature" (RSV). Psalm 82:6 also was influential: "You are gods . . . sons of the Most High."

In the light of this type of biblical background, Athanasius

(c. 296-373 felt able to make such statements as, "The Word became man so that we might be deified" (i.e., made like God), and, "The Son of God became man so as to deify us in himself." That he saw sonship and deification as identical comes across in the statement, "By becoming man he made us sons to the Father, and he deified men by himself becoming man."[4] More clearly, his belief that salvation is only enjoyed by those who are united to Christ is seen in this statement:

> This is God's loving-kindness to men, that by grace he becomes the Father of those whose Creator he already is. This comes about when created men, as the apostle says, receive the Spirit of his Son crying, "Abba, Father," in their hearts. It is these who, receiving the Spirit, have obtained power from him to become God's children. Being creatures by nature, they would never have become sons if they had not received the Spirit from him who is true Son by nature.[5]

Thus we may grow into closer communion with God through Christ and become less attached to and dominated by those forces in the universe which cause alienation and disorder. This is the process of becoming genuinely human, if being human is seen in the light of Christ, the perfect man.

Augustine's contribution to these concepts was to emphasize the love of God in the human heart reaching out to God and neighbor.

Augustine of Hippo (354-430)[6]

Some of Augustine's writings—e.g., *Confessions* and *City of God*—rank among the classics of Western literature. His influence on the course of theology after his death was immense. The shape of medieval theology and aspects of Reformation theology were molded by his teaching. In fact, the development of Western theology owed more to St. Augustine than to any other theologian.

He applied his great intellect and spiritual perception to many issues. The problem that required his attention during the last twenty years of his life was the Pelagian controversy. Pelagius, a British theologian who was teaching in Rome, had taken offense at Augustine's famous remark in his *Confessions:* "Grant what thou dost command, and command what thou wilt" (X.29).[7] Pelagius claimed that the will of every human being was free to obey God's will. Sin had not affected the freedom of the will either to choose or do the divine will. To Augustine and others, the religion of Pelagius appeared to be a religion without grace. Augustine used the teachings of Paul to show the errors and heresy of Pelagianism, and in so doing he expounded his doctrine of justification, along with related doctrines of the freedom of the will and the place of moral law.

Augustine wrote a great deal, but only some of his writings have been translated into English from the original Latin. Happily, the clearest statement of his response to Pelagianism occurs in *The Spirit and the Letter,* and this is available in translation.[8] The teaching of Augustine on justification may be briefly stated as follows:

1. *The justice/righteousness of God in the teaching of Paul is not an attribute of God, but that by which he justifies and gives salvation to the sinner.* He made much use of the epistle to the Romans, where the gospel is said to be the power of God unto salvation because in the gospel the righteousness of God is revealed (1:17; 3:21). Contrary to Pelagian exegesis, Augustine maintained that "the righteousness of God (is) not that by which God is righteous, but that wherewith he clothes man, when he justifies the ungodly."[9] He believed it "was hidden in the Old Testament and revealed in the New: called the righteousness of God, because by imparting it God makes man righteous."[10] This righteousness brings salvation because it is of God and through Jesus Christ, Savior and Mediator.

2. *To justify means to make righteous.* The Latin term *justificatio* is postclassical, so no readily available interpretation existed. Augustine decided that *justificari* means "to make righteous," thereby apparently treating *-ficari* as the unstressed form of *facere,* as in *sanctificatio, vivificatio* and *glorificatio.* He held that the sinner is actually made righteous in justification.[11] He briefly considered and rejected the possibility that "to justify" could mean "to pronounce righteous" (Section 45).

He wrote of righteousness as an internal gift of God. "Man is justified by the gift of God through the help of the Spirit." "God confers righteousness upon the believer through the Spirit of grace." And, "This is the Spirit of God by whose gift we are justified."[12]

3. *Justification describes the whole Christian life. It is both the initial event and the continuing process throughout life, leading to the perfect righteousness of the eternal kingdom of God.* Justification is an event in and through baptism, at which time God forgives sin. Thereafter it is the internal growth of righteousness in the life of the believing sinner. In a sermon on Romans 8 Augustine said: "We have been justified; but this justice increases, as we make advance. And how it increases I will say, and so to say confer with you, that each one of you, already established in this justification, having received to wit the remission of sins by the laver of regeneration (= baptism), having received the Holy Ghost, making advancement from day to day, may see where he is, may go on, advance, and grow, till he be consummated, not so as to come to an end, but to perfection."[13]

At the close of *The Spirit and the Letter,* Augustine wrote:

It follows, as I see it, that in whatever kind or degree we may define righteousness in this life, there is in this life no man entirely without sin: there is need for every man to give that it may be given to him, to forgive that it may be forgiven him, and in respect of any righteousness he possesses not to presume that it has come of his own making, but to accept it as of the grace of God who justifies; yet none the less to hunger and thirst for the gift of righteousness from him who is the living bread and with whom is the well of life—who so works justification in his saints that labor in the trial of this life, that there is always somewhat his bounty may add in answer to their prayer, or his goodness pardon upon their confession.[14]

To enter into the righteousness of the eternal kingdom, Augustine believed, the believer needed to persevere to the end of this life in faith and love.

When commenting on the book of Psalms he wrote: "He alone justifies who, by himself and not by another, is just. It is God who justifies, and . . . by justifying them he makes them sons of God. If we have become sons of God . . . this is due to gratuitous adoption, and not natural generation."[15]

4. *Justification is by faith and love.* While Augustine often declared that justification is by faith, he much preferred to say that justification is by faith and love, or by love alone. This is because he took faith to be the act of believing in the sense of accepting the gospel on the authority of the Church which taught it. Such faith needed love, in terms of love of God and of neighbor, so that it was not merely a dead faith or a faith such as devils possess. Augustine wrote: "By the faith of Jesus Christ—the faith, that is, which Christ has conferred upon us—we believe that from God is given to us, and will be given yet more fully, the life of righteousness." And, "The man in whom is the faith that works through love (Gal. 5:6) begins to delight in the law of God after the inward man; and that delight is a gift not of the letter but of the Spirit." Also, "And this is the gift of the Holy Spirit, by which charity is shed abroad in our hearts; that charity alone which is the love of God from a pure heart and a good conscience and a faith unfeigned (1 Tim. 1:5)."[16] For Augustine, *amor* (love) is a neutral term. When directed towards God it becomes *charitas* (charity). True righteousness is found when *amor* as *charitas* is directed to God and neighbor.

5. *The grace of God prepares the will of man for justification and strengthens the will in justification.* Augustine made the distinction between operative grace working before justification and cooperative grace working in the justified believer. The question of the freedom of the will was at the center of the Pelagian controversy. Augustine held that each man has free will but does not possess the liberty to function properly. Man as a sinner is incapacitated and needs the help of divine grace both to believe and to make progress in Christian commitment and life. The grace of God heals the free will so that it has true liberty to believe the gospel and to love God and neighbor. As the Bishop of Hippo remarked: "Not that the justification is without our will, but the weakness of our will is discovered by the law, so that grace may restore the will and the restored will may fulfil the law, established neither

under the law nor in need of law."[17] And he also wrote: "As the law is not made void by faith, so freedom of choice is not made void but established by grace. Freedom of choice is necessary to the fulfillment of the law. But by the law comes the knowledge of sin; by faith comes the obtaining of grace against sin; by grace comes the healing of the soul from sin's sickness; by the healing of the soul comes freedom of choice; by freedom of choice comes the love of righteousness; by the love of righteousness comes the working of the law."[18] So grace establishes liberty or freedom of choice and then assists liberty to achieve righteousness. Having a good will and moving with that will into good acts of love—this is righteousness.

It will be seen that while Augustine teaches the nonimputation of sin (= forgiveness from God) he does not teach the imputation of righteousness, as did Luther and Protestantism after him. Protestant writers from the sixteenth to the twentieth century have tried to find in Augustine the same doctrine of justification as is found in the Protestant confessions of the Reformation period.[19] It has to be admitted that the great theologian of grace does not teach a "Protestant" doctrine of justification. In fact, Augustine never had more than a minimal knowledge of the Greek language and was therefore unable seriously to face the question of what *dikaioō* meant for St. Paul. Thus his legacy to the Latin West, which is still to be found in the Roman Catholic Church, is the interpretation of justification as both an event and process of making the unrighteous man into a righteous man.

St. Thomas Aquinas (c. 1225-1274)

Declared "Doctor of the Church" by Pope Pius V in 1567, Aquinas still warrants careful study. His influence, especially over Roman Catholic theology, has been immense. He was both a philosopher and theologian and may be said to have baptized Aristotelian philosophy for use in the systematic presentation of Christian truth.[20]

Many Protestant students find it difficult to begin to read Aquinas. This is in part because his name is associated in much traditional Protestant thinking with salvation by works. It is also because his style, with its use of Aristotelian categories, seems so far removed from the dynamic and common-sense language of the Bible. It must be admitted that there is no easy way to understand Aquinas, but those who do persevere will realize, perhaps to their surprise, that he is a theologian of grace who certainly does not teach that we receive eternal life by human achievement.

The question of justification was treated by Aquinas at three points in his voluminous writings. First he discussed it in the context of the sacrament of penance in his *Commentary on the Sentences of Peter Lombard,* written between 1252 and 1256. This needs a brief explanation. The beginning of justification as the process of making righteous was seen as taking place at baptism. But what happened to justification when the person in the process of being made righteous committed sin?

This is where the practice of private confession to a priest came in.[21] The restoration of justification, or the reentry into the process of being made righteous, was seen as being effected by the grace of God through the use of the sacrament of penance, involving certain acts of the penitent and the absolution of the priest. So not only was the process of justification clearly linked with one sacrament; it was also placed definitely within the structures of the Church. Aquinas accepted this development even though, we can see now, it meant that the more dynamic idea of being made righteous, as presented by Augustine, was in danger of being lost as the process of growth in righteousness was made dependent on sacraments whose validity was guaranteed by the Church. The Protestant Reformation can be interpreted, in part, as a rejection of such a close identification.

The relation of justification to the sacraments of the Church is also dealt with by Aquinas in his *Quaestiones Disputatae de Veritate,* dating from 1256 to 1259. Baptism is the sacrament by which justification is begun, with the sacraments of penance and holy communion contributing to the process of justification.

His most mature discussion of the topic is to be found in the *Summa Theologiae.* Here it is not treated with reference to the sacraments but in the treatise on grace in the *Seconda Pars,* which traces the essential structure of the return of the sinner to God. In this approach Aquinas was adopting the method of theologians in the thirteenth century and seeking to bring clarity to the relation of the grace of God and human choice.

We shall be describing the view of Aquinas as it appears in the *Summa Theologiae.* The reader is invited to look carefully at the answer to question 113 as found in 1a2ae (Blackfriars edition, Vol. 30). First, however, a brief statement of his doctrine of grace (questions 109-112) will be helpful.

1. *Grace is given to man wholly from outside man.* Grace is the result of the presence and work of the Holy Spirit, who operates in the name of Jesus Christ. As such grace cannot be earned or merited, it always remains the gift of God and the initiative of God.

2. *Grace is infused into the essence of the soul and dwells habitually there.* Grace does not mean that a new nature or new potentialities as such are given to the soul. While grace and the human soul are different substances, grace is so present in the soul as to be called a *habit* or permanent disposition, which becomes the root or source of the virtues of faith, hope and love. Grace is also a *quality* in the soul in that it causes the soul to exist in a different way. Grace is also an *accidental form* of the soul in that while the substance of the soul remains what it always has been, grace gives it a purpose and meaning which belong not to the finite but to the infinite world.

3. *Grace is not necessary for man to fulfill his role and purpose in nature as a man; but it is necessary for him to attain eternal life.* As a creature, each human being has been given by God a purpose and an

end within the created order. This includes a moral and spiritual perfection which belongs to man as an intelligent being. But it is a perfection within the finite, created order. Grace is not concerned primarily with making it possible for man to attain his natural end, but is rather concerned with making it possible for man to obtain the true vision of God with eternal life in Heaven. Had Adam not sinned, he would still have needed grace to cause him to be able to enter Heaven since even perfect or perfected human nature cannot gain entrance to Heaven on its own merits.

4. *While grace has the effect of renewing and restoring the soul (which is impaired by sin), its primary purpose is to elevate the soul.* The soul needs to be lifted into a higher plane of existence if it is to move towards the gates of Heaven and thus have a supernatural goal. Knowledge of such a goal is the gift of God by revelation and illumination, and the entrance into and the journey along the road to that goal is the gift of God's grace. Grace elevates the soul to a plane at whose end is the true vision of God.

5. *Grace is both beyond nature and in accordance with nature.* God is the only source of grace and only he (normally via the sacraments) can infuse grace into the soul. So grace is beyond or outside nature in its origin and its essence. However, once infused, grace works within the soul, causing what is within the soul to move towards a different goal. Grace enables the soul and its powers of mind and will to move towards a supernatural goal. So it may be said to be acting within the soul in accordance with nature in that it causes only the elevation of the soul, not a change in the makeup of the soul. This is why salvation is said to be not the fulfillment of creation but the transcending of creation, for grace heightens or elevates the image and likeness of God within man so that it is directed towards God himself in his glory.

6. *Grace is presented in ontological rather than psychological terms.* Augustine saw grace as the activity of God healing and restoring the human motivation and will to their proper functions of loving God and neighbor (righteousness). Without denying these effects of grace. Aquinas described grace primarily in ontological terms. Grace elevates the soul to a new plane of existence; grace gives the soul a supernatural end and goal. Here, of course, is the influence of the Aristotelian categories which he adopted. The effect of the method of Aquinas is to offer a description of the dynamic experience of Christians (their life as disciples of Christ and servants of God) in nondynamic and nonexistential terms. Because his theology is so divorced from experience, many have found it (and the systems which have developed from it) hard to understand or to accept. Among these we must name Martin Luther.

7. *Grace both justifies and sanctifies the sinner.* Justification *(justificatio)* is presented as a process. It is a passing from a state of sin to a state of righteousness/justice. It is a movement from one state of being to another state. Sanctification *(sanctificatio)* is another way of describing the same process in terms of a deepening participation in the divine

life through the presence of infused grace in the soul. As grace elevates and heightens the soul, it causes it to participate in the love of God.

Thus it can be seen that despite (what may seem to many moderns) the unhelpful use of Aristotelian categories/words, Aquinas emphasizes that without grace there is no possibility of gaining eternal life. Turning in more detail to his doctrine of justification we find the same clear emphasis.

We must remember that (from a post-sixteenth century perspective) Aquinas's discussion of justification is limited to what was called the *processus justificationis* (the process of justification), which had been defined as a theological topic for debate for about a century. While agreeing with his contemporaries that justification was the process of making just/righteous, he offered his own solution to this restricted theological problem of the process of justification. So his view of justification may be stated as follows.

8. *The justification of the unrighteous is the effect of operative grace.* God alone causes the beginning of the process of justification. God is the supernatural Mover, and the unrighteous are those who are moved to will the good (having previously willed that which did not please God). In question 111, article 2 Aquinas makes it very clear that no man can merit justification, for God alone can and does cause the process to begin. This particular action of God as Mover is called operative grace *(gratia operans)*.

9. *Justification is so named because it is the process whereby unrighteous man comes to possess supernatural justice* (question 113, article 1). Aquinas carefully distinguished between human justice on the one hand and divine or supernatural or infused (or "metaphorical" in the Aristotelian sense) justice on the other. It is the work of the Holy Spirit to infuse supernatural justice into the human soul. It is the gift of God, the result of his operative grace, and it becomes the possession (since it is within the soul) of the baptized Christian.

10. *Considered as a process or movement, justification may be said to have four logically distinct elements.* Using the analogy of physical movement, he listed four requirements for the justification of the sinner. These are "the infusion of grace; a movement of free choice directed towards God by faith; a movement of free choice directed towards sin; and the forgiveness of sin" (question 113, article 6). This whole process is the result of operative grace, and it involves both a right relationship with God and the right ordering of the Christian life towards the love and obedience of God. The elements of this process can be discussed from various perspectives—temporal succession, logical sequence and human experience. What matters is that all four must be recognized.

It has rightly been said that "God's gracious action upon us (according to Aquinas) is unique and unified in its origin and its ultimate goal (but) diversified in its effects in our plural, complex and evolving reality" as Christian believers.[22]

11. *Within the process of justification the baptized Christian may gain merit through the effect of cooperative grace (gratia cooperans).* Aquinas quoted Augustine with approval: "By his cooperation (with us) God perfects in us what he initiates by his operation; since by his operation he initiates our willing who, by his cooperation with us who will, perfects us" (question 111, article 2).[23] Having made a clear distinction between operative grace and cooperative grace, the one initiating and the other continuing the process of justification, Aquinas went on to discuss merit as the effect of cooperative grace.

Aquinas held that while man cannot merit grace, he can in a state of grace and with the help of grace gain merit before God by his cooperation with God and his use of the grace given to him by God (question 114). Merit is based on God's free decision in grace to reward baptized believers who seek to do his will. The biblical background to this is the teaching in the New Testament on rewards in the Kingdom of Heaven (see e.g., Matt. 5:12, 46; 6:1; 10:41, 42). In fact, Aquinas taught nothing new in this area and differs little from Augustine who said: "The merits of man are the gifts of God, and God does not crown your merits as your merits, but as his gifts."[24] Such teaching is fine when it is clearly expounded and clearly understood. Regrettably it has often been so taught or so received that it appears to produce a doctrine of salvation by works or by human effort. Certainly thousands of Protestants have understood Aquinas and the tradition of theology connected with him in this light.

After the time of Aquinas the doctrine of justification continued to be discussed in the different schools of medieval theology—e.g., Dominican and Franciscan. While differences of approach and method may certainly be detected, it is clear that the discussion remains within the general principle that "to justify is to make righteous." As yet the idea that to justify is to declare or pronounce righteous has not appeared and will not appear until Luther. Thus the search for forerunners of the Reformers—that is, men (heretic or orthodox) who actually taught the Reformation doctrine of justification—has produced none and seems incapable of producing any.[25]

6 The Lutheran View

Of all churches it is the Lutheran which is most obviously associated with the doctrine of justification by faith. And for good reason. It was Luther who introduced the doctrine into the postmedièval Church. So our study begins with him.

Martin Luther (1483-1546)[1]

As both a personality and a writer, Luther raises deep feelings in many of us. He spoke from the heart with passion, but he did so via a powerful intellect. He was full of new ideas which were often expressed imprecisely. To interpret his thought and to present it systematically is a fascinating but difficult task. What he says about justification is clear in its outlines but sometimes apparently contradictory in details. It is found scattered in many rich writings, belonging to a period of thirty or so years. Perhaps the English-speaking student will most profitably encounter it in the translations of his *Preface to the Epistle to the Romans* (1515), *The Freedom of a Christian Man* (1520) and *Commentary on Galatians* (1535). These have often been reprinted and are available in a variety of editions.

Luther's doctrine may be described as a restatement of the teaching of St. Augustine of Hippo in the light of his study of the letters of St. Paul (especially that to Rome). It became for him the article of faith by which the Church stands or falls. He saw the doctrine as contained in the whole of the Bible while recognizing that St. Paul gave it particular clarity in his controversy with Judaizers in Galatia and in his exposition of the gospel addressed to the Roman church. He made the teaching the foundation of his ethics.[2] By this doctrine he challenged the Pope and the Church of Rome, and in the light of it he called for the reformation of the whole Church.

Luther saw this doctrine as the expression of the gospel. It brought together the God of grace and sinful, condemned man. It asserted that salvation is wholly by divine mercy and of the divine initiative; God in Christ has made salvation possible. Justification rests wholly on the grace of God revealed and given to sinful man in Jesus Christ, Savior and Mediator. That grace is desperately needed is seen in the position of human beings. Not only are they guilty before God, the just judge, in that they have broken his moral law, but they are also totally unable to help themselves since they possess an enslaved will. They can do nothing whatsoever to merit or gain salvation, for they are in bondage to sin. This is the theme of Luther's book, *The Bondage of the Will* (1525).[3]

Luther believed doctrine and personal experience cannot be separated. Justification by faith arose as a clear concept in his mind after a long and painful search for a gracious God who would accept him as he was rather than condemn him for his sins. This absorbing search involved his whole self and included meticulous study of the Scriptures and consultation of the works of the Fathers. In particular it involved a study of the meaning of the righteousness/justice of God as Paul uses the expression in the letter to the Romans, especially in 1:16, 17—"For I am not ashamed of the gospel of Christ: for it is the power of God unto salvation to every one that believeth; to the Jew first, and also to the Greek. For therein is the righteousness of God revealed from faith to faith: as it is written, 'The just shall live by faith' " (KJV). Luther explained:

> I greatly longed to understand Paul's Epistle to the Romans and nothing stood in the way but one expression, "the justice of God," because I took it to mean that justice whereby God is just and deals justly in punishing the unjust. My situation was that, although an impeccable monk, I stood before God as a sinner troubled in conscience, and I had no confidence that my merit would assuage him. Therefore I did not love a just and angry God, but rather hated and murmured against him. Yet I clung to the dear Paul and had a great yearning to know what he meant.
>
> Night and day I pondered until I saw the connection between the justice of God and the statement that "the just shall live by his faith." Then I grasped that the justice of God is that righteousness by which through grace and sheer mercy God justifies us through faith. Thereupon I felt myself to be reborn and to have gone through open doors into paradise. The whole of Scripture took on a new meaning, and whereas before the "justice of God" had filled me with hate, now it became to me inexpressibly sweet in great love. This passage of Paul became to me a gate to heaven.[4]

It hardly needs adding that this discovery changed the direction of his life and led to his becoming an outstanding reformer of the Church.[5]

In fact, as Luther later realized, Augustine and many other writers had presented God's justice (as found in Paul's theology) not in terms of an attribute of God but as his saving and justifying activity.

It is tempting to comment on his fascinating career as a reformer but our task is to state and examine the explanation of justification which he offered not once but many times in his voluminous writings. His doctrine represented a major innovation and development in terms of the history of the doctrine of justification in the Western Church.[6] It may also be claimed that his exposition reached a high point that his successors never quite reached. Our method will be to offer various headings and then explain each one.

1. *The message of justification is the word of the gospel.* The righteousness of God is the saving activity of God in Christ by the Holy Spirit. Thus righteousness is the foundation and the explanation of the gospel. When the good news is declared as the word of God, the gospel (by the Holy Spirit acting in the name of Christ) creates faith in the hearts of its hearers. God's righteousness is that by which the gospel effectively creates true faith and establishes the state of being justified by faith. It is all of grace, from beginning to end. As an article of belief, justification by faith cannot be overestimated. As Luther wrote in the Schmalkaldic Articles of 1537: "Nothing in this article can be given up or compromised, even if Heaven and earth and things temporal should be destroyed. . . . On this article rests all that we teach and practice against the pope, and devil and the world. Therefore we must be quite certain and have no doubts about it. Otherwise all is lost and the pope, the devil and all our adversaries will gain the victory."[7]

2. *Justification is entirely based on the alien righteousness of the living Christ, the same yesterday, today and forever.* It is an alien righteousness in the sense that it never belongs personally to the sinner; it is totally different from and contrary to his own (un)righteousness, and it belongs entirely and always to Jesus Christ. As Luther said: "Christ or Christ's righteousness is outside of us and alien . . . to us." And, "To be outside of us means to be beyond our powers. Righteousness is our possession, to be sure, since it was given to us out of mercy. Nevertheless it is alien to us, because we have not merited it." And, "This is a peculiar righteousness: it is strange indeed that we are to be called righteous or to possess a righteousness which is in us but is entirely outside us in Christ and yet becomes our very own, as though we ourselves had achieved and earned it."[8] There is a wonderful exchange by which our sins are no longer ours but Christ's, and Christ's righteousness no longer his alone but also ours.

In *The Freedom of a Christian Man* Luther wrote: "Because Christ is God and man, and has never sinned, and because his sanctity is unconquerable, eternal and almighty, he takes possession of the sins of the believing soul by virtue of her wedding-ring, namely faith, and acts just as if he had committed those sins himself. They are, of course, swallowed up and drowned in him, for his unconquerable righteous-

ness is stronger than any sin whatever. Thus the soul is cleansed from
all her sins by virtue of her dowry, that is, for the sake of her faith. She
is made free and unfettered, and endowed with the eternal righteousness of Christ, her bridegroom."[9]

It is important to note that Luther does not employ forensic terms
to explain this imputation of alien righteousness. This development
will come later, from others.

3. *Justification is received in the form of faith since God justifies a
sinner by giving him faith.* Man possesses an enslaved will with sin as
his master. Faith must be, and is, the gift of God, created by the power
of God within the gospel. Luther makes clear that faith cannot be
defined merely as assent to what the Church teaches or what the Bible
says. It is not an idea in the head without a corresponding experience in
the depths of the heart. Both the mind and will must turn to Christ in
order to apprehend him.

Faith grasps Christ, appropriates him and makes him my own.
This is *fides apprehensiva.* This means that Christ is not only the object
of my faith but is also present in my faith. In this spiritual union the
sinner participates in the righteousness of Christ and is justified.

Once true faith had been created by the word of the gospel, it
expresses itself dynamically. As Luther wrote in *Preface to the Epistle to
the Romans:*

> Faith, however, is something that God effects in us. It changes us
> and we are reborn from God, John 1:13. Faith puts the old Adam
> to death and makes us quite different men in heart, in mind, and
> in all our powers; and it is accompanied by the Holy Spirit. O,
> when it comes to faith, what a living, creative, active, powerful
> thing it is. It cannot do other than good at all times. It never waits
> to ask whether there is some good work to do; rather, before the
> question is raised, it has done the deed, and keeps on doing it. A
> man not active in this way is a man without faith. He is groping
> about for faith and searching for good works, but knows neither
> what faith is nor what good works are. Nevertheless, he keeps on
> talking nonsense about faith and good works.[10]

In the light of these explanatory comments on the nature of faith, it
will be recognized that to say *sola fide* is in fact to say that salvation is by
grace alone. Because of his rich understanding of "faith" Luther only
needs to say "justification by faith."

4. *Justification by faith is both an event and a process.* What later
Protestants were to divide, Luther kept together. He was quite clear
that there is a moment when the sinner is actually justified by faith. He
then has the righteousness of another, the alien righteousness of Christ,
imputed to him. But this is the beginning of a journey towards a time
(following the resurrection of the dead in the age to come) when he
will in fact possess a perfect righteousness created in him by the Spirit
of God. "For we perceive that a man who is justified is not yet a

righteous man, but is in the very movement or journey towards righteousness." And, "Our justification is not yet complete . . . . It is still under construction. It shall, however, be completed in the resurrection of the dead."[11] It is an event and process because faith, the gift of God, receives both the forgiveness of sins through the imputation of righteousness and also in the Spirit creates the new nature, the very nature which finds its fulfillment in the resurrection body.

5. *Justification by faith means that the Christian is simultaneously sinful and just (simul iustus et peccator).* While on earth, the position of the Christian does not change. He is totally righteous through faith, and he remains always and completely a sinner. With reference to Christ he is righteous; but with reference to his fallen nature he is sinful. Yet this apparent contradiction does not imply a static situation. The very faith that draws Christ into the heart and creates the new nature gladly and freely allows Christ to do battle against the old, sinful nature (= "the flesh"). The result of this spiritual conflict (described by St. Paul in Romans 7, 8) should be that "Christ is constantly formed in us and we are formed according to his own image."[12] Each and every day faith is to grasp anew the word of promise which is the gospel and appropriate Christ, who is our righteousness. Further, each and every day sin, the devil and temptation must be fought. Yet despite all the daily battles, the old nature remains with us until death. There is no escape from it, nor from the possibility of sin. So Luther has no doctrine of progressive holiness or growth in sanctification (as these terms were later used). The flesh or old nature does not change; rather, Christ (or really the new nature) grows within the believer. Justification includes the daily renewal of the new nature. The believer can never say he is less sinful than he was at any earlier time!

6. *Justification by faith leads the Christian to love his neighbor in a genuine and practical manner.* Because justification includes the creation of a new nature within the sinner, there is in him a new principle of divine love. Thus faith naturally seeks out the neighbor to love him.

> Faith is a living and unshakeable confidence, a belief in the grace of God so assured that a man would die a thousand deaths for its sake. This kind of confidence in God's grace, this sort of knowledge of it, makes us joyful, high-spirited, and eager in our relations with God and with all mankind. That is what the Holy Spirit effects through faith. Hence, the man of faith, without being driven, willingly and gladly seeks to do good to everyone, serve everyone, suffer all kinds of hardships, for the sake of the love and glory of the God who has shown him such grace. It is impossible, indeed, to separate works from faith, just as it is impossible to separate heat and light from fire.[13]

The second part of *The Freedom of a Christian Man* is devoted to establishing the truth of the statement that "a Christian is a dutiful servant in every respect, owing a duty to everyone." Luther was quite clear that good works do not save a man from sin; but he was also quite clear that a justified man will perform good works for God's glory and the benefit of mankind.

7. *Justification by faith is paradoxical and contrary to reason.* Luther held that God, as judge, was obliged to require perfect obedience to his law from his creatures and to punish them if they did not offer that obedience. The idea that they should be accepted by God because of an alien righteousness was at best paradoxical and at worst irrational. So in this area of doctrine, as in others, Luther delighted to affirm that the God of revelation and salvation, and thus the God who justifies, acts contrary to human reason. "Human nature, corrupt and blinded by the blemish of original sin, is not able to imagine or conceive of any justification above and beyond works."[14] Not all Luther's successors accepted his position. In the period of Lutheran orthodoxy, theologians saw reason as a handmaid for the gospel and produced what may be called rational accounts of the doctrine of justification.

Having claimed that Luther's doctrine was a restatement with modifications of Augustine's teaching, we are now in a position to note what are those modifications. Further it will be helpful to note the major differences between Aquinas and Luther.

Augustine, Aquinas and Luther

Following his discovery of the meaning of righteousness in Romans 1:17, Luther read Augustine and was conscious that they did not wholly agree. In his enigmatic "Autobiographical Fragment" he wrote:

> Later I read Augustine on *The Spirit and the Letter,* where beyond all hope I found that he also interprets the righteousness of God in the same way, as that in which God clothes us when he justifies us. And although Augustine's statement is still open to criticism, and he is neither clear nor comprehensive in the matter of imputation, yet he is satisfied that the righteousness of God should be taught to be that by which we are justified.[15]

Luther certainly followed the bishop of Hippo in understanding the righteousness of God to mean the gracious, saving activity of God rather than an eternal attribute of God. Also they were agreed in seeing justification as a description of the whole Christian life, covering the relation of the soul to God as well as the renewal of the inner man.

But Luther saw the basis of justification in the alien righteousness of Christ *(justitia extra nos),* while Augustine located it within an internal, infused righteousness *(justitia in nobis).* They agreed that sin is not imputed to the believer and so justification includes forgiveness. Luther looked to the righteousness of Christ, who is always at God's right hand but present in the Spirit. In contrast, Augustine looked to the righteousness actually imparted to the believer through the presence of the Spirit. So Luther talked of the imputed alien (external) righteousness of Christ; concerning this Augustine had nothing to say, for his emphasis was on the internal righteousness caused by the Spirit.

Secondly, Luther saw no progression within the internal aspect of justification because the old nature remains fundamentally the same, with the human will always enslaved to sin. In contrast, Augustine believed that the Christian is actually in a process of becoming righteous, with his will liberated by the Spirit so that his old nature can be renewed and perfected. For Luther, the all-important fact is the presence of Christ by the Spirit bringing his own life into the soul, that life being the new nature. Augustine, in contrast, saw the divine life as permeating and thus becoming in some sense the possession of the soul, so that the soul can grow in righteousness.

It is much more difficult to compare Aquinas and Luther. This is because their approaches are so very different. Otto Pesch has referred to the contrast of a "sapiential" and an "existential" theology.[16] Luther described the position of the human being before God in personal and relational categories. In a personal relationship with God, experience affirms that sin and grace are not exclusive or even contradictory. Grace exists despite and because of human sinfulness. There is no absurdity in affirming *simul justus et peccator.*

In contrast, Aquinas, who offered a coherent explanation of the relation of a human being to God through objective, metaphysical causes, saw sin and grace to be exclusive categories. It is metaphysically and ontologically absurd to state that a person is in sin and in grace (righteousness) at the same time. Thus *simul justus et peccator* seemed to Roman Catholics who followed the general scheme of Aquinas to be quite ridiculous. In fact, it is the methodological differences which make it difficult to contrast what the two great men say about any aspect of doctrine—that of merit for example.[17]

Philipp Melanchthon (1497-1560)[18]

Luther and Melanchthon had very different personalities and backgrounds, but they worked together for reform in Germany. Whereas Luther was bold, impulsive, innovative and controversial, Melanchthon was calm, cool, rational and conciliatory. The former had been an Augustinian monk, whereas the latter had been and remained a humanist scholar. From Melanchthon came the first ordered presentation of Protestant (Lutheran) doctrine in the often reprinted *Loci Communes* (1521).[19] Besides his biblical commentaries, he was also the primary writer of the *Augsburg Confession* (1530) and its *Apology.*[20]

The assumption that Luther and Melanchthon used identical thought patterns and imagery is misleading. Certainly there were important and striking similarities in their use of language, but there were also differences. (These differences were perhaps less significant at the time than they are now as we consider the development of doctrine with the benefit of hindsight.)

What Melanchthon wrote in the *Loci* (1521) about justification is in full accord with Luther's teaching, though perhaps not having the same richness.

> Therefore, we are justified when, put to death by the law, we are made alive again by the word of grace promised in Christ; the gospel forgives our sins, and we cling to Christ in faith, not doubting in the least that the righteousness of Christ is our righteousness, that the satisfaction Christ wrought is our expiation, and that the resurrection of Christ is ours. In a word, we do not doubt at all that our sins have been forgiven and that God now favors us and wills our good. Nothing, therefore, of our own works, however good they may seem or be, constitutes our righteousness. But *faith* alone in the mercy and grace of God in Christ Jesus is our *righteousness*. This is what the prophet says and what Paul discusses so often. "The righteous shall live by faith" (Rom. 1:17).
>
> Why is it that justification is attributed to faith alone? I answer that since we are justified by the mercy of God alone, and faith is clearly the recognition of that mercy by whatever promise you apprehend it, justification is attributed to faith alone. Let those who marvel that justification is attributed to faith alone marvel also that justification is attributed only to the mercy of God, and not rather to human merits. For to trust in divine mercy is to have no confidence in any of our own works. He who denies that the saints are justified by faith offends against divine mercy. For since our justification is a work of divine mercy alone and is not a merit of our own works, as Paul clearly teaches in Romans, chapter 11, justification must be attributed to faith alone; faith is that through which alone we receive the promised mercy.[21]

The differences in expression and figurative structure between Melanchthon and Luther begin to surface in the text of the *Augsburg Confession* and its *Apology*. The former reads:

IV. Of Justification.

> They teach that men cannot be justified in the sight of God by their own strength, merits or works, but that they are justified freely on account of Christ through faith, when they believe that they are received into grace and that their sins are remitted on account of Christ who made satisfaction for sins on our behalf by his death. God imputes this faith for righteousness in his own sight (Romans iii and iv).

Here it may be noted that justification is expressed in forensic terms. This is clear in the Latin text, *propter Christum per fidem* (on account of Christ through faith). Whereas Luther consistently used personal images of relationship (e.g., bride and bridegroom) to describe the union of Christ and the sinner in which the alien righteousness of Christ is imputed to the sinner, Melanchthon (followed by others) began to use words and images—"pronouncement," "acceptation," "forensic"—taken from Roman law. God the judge pronounces sentence and declares that *on account of* the righteousness of another (Christ) the believing sinner is to be reckoned or accounted as righteous. In the *Apology* there are the following statements:

"To be justified does not mean that a wicked man is made righteous, but that he is pronounced righteous forensically" (Art. IV, 252); "It is faith, therefore, which God declares to be righteousness: St. Paul adds that it is accounted freely and denies that it could be accounted freely if it were a reward for works" (Art. IV, 89).

The understanding of imputation in a forensic sense was to increase as Melanchthon and others did battle with Osiander (whose views are discussed below). Though the change in the type of illustrative image may seem minor, it did have within it the possibility of viewing justification not as a statement of a God-created union of Christ and the sinner for the latter's salvation, but rather as one of the blessings or benefits earned for his people by Christ.[22]

Another difference must also be noted. Whereas for Luther justification included regeneration and renewal, for Melanchthon (and the majority of orthodox Lutheran and Reformed protestants after him) justification came to be seen as only the declaration by God that a sinner is reckoned righteous. R. S. Franks has commented that Melanchthon sowed the seeds of a return to the analytic methods of the medieval schoolmen: "Above all justification and regeneration, the forgiveness of sins and the gift of the Spirit are carefully separated."[23] This conceptual distinction between justification and regeneration/sanctification came to assume great importance, especially after it was adopted by John Calvin. That Melanchthon could hold to such a distinction as well as teach forensic justification makes even stranger his claim that he taught the same doctrine of justification as Augustine.[24]

The same analytic methods to which Franks refers were used by Melanchthon to decide at what point in the process of psychological-religious experience God actually declares that the sinner is righteous. This tendency is seen in the revised edition of the *Loci* (1535) and especially in the third edition of 1543. How do the Word of God (proclaimed from Scripture), the power of the Spirit and the human will relate to each other in the process of conversion and in the declaration of justification? This question is related to the problem of the *ordo salutis,* with which Lutheran dogmaticians came to be concerned (see below). For Luther, the basic element in all false religion was the idea: "If I do thus and so, God will be merciful to me." By making the movement of the human will or faith (or both) in some sense or another a cause of justification or as preceding justification, Melanchthon was testifying that the insight of Luther was being lost!

Andreas Osiander (1498-1552)[25]

Osiander joined the Lutherans in 1522 and in 1549 became professor at Königsberg, the place where his *De Justificatione* was published in 1550. His teaching caused controversy with Lutheranism and was deemed sufficiently important and erroneous by Calvin for him to condemn it in his *Institutes*.

The doctrine of Osiander appeared at first sight to be similar to that taught by Luther as well as by Augustine. Justification was only by grace received in faith. But he had no use for the idea that the righteousness by which the sinner is justified is either external or forensic. It was his view that it must be internal, and he located it within Christ himself who is made present in the soul through the Spirit, the Paraclete of Christ. However, and here he differed from Augustine, he meant by righteousness not what had come to be called the mediatorial righteousness of Christ, but rather his essential attribute as the eternal *righteous* Son of God. Thus, with Luther and Augustine, he accepted that justification is both the forgiveness of sins and the renewal of the soul; against Luther, he maintained that the righteousness was imparted not imputed; and against both Luther and Augustine, he maintained that the righteousness was only that of the divine nature of Christ. To add to the picture, against Melanchthon and other Lutherans, he denied forensic (imputed) righteousness. Thus he was vulnerable for criticism from many sides.

It is often the case that one extreme generates its opposite. Francesco Stancaro, an Italian, opposed Osiander in Königsberg by affirming that the righteousness of Christ by which we are justified is located only in his human nature. So later it was necessary in the *Formula of Concord* to affirm that the righteousness of Christ belongs to him as one person with two natures.

The Formula of Concord (1577)[26]

The controversy involving Osiander and Stancaro was not the only one within Lutheranism. There were others involving the questions of justification and good works and the ability or inability of the sinner to say yes or no to the call of God in the gospel. One major purpose of the *Formula of Concord* was to find a solution to the various theological disagreements within the Lutheran churches. This purpose was achieved at a time when the decrees and canons of the Council of Trent (1545-1563) on justification and other disputed areas were known. So while the *Formula* is primarily addressed to Lutheran disputes, it does so in the context of what was declared at Trent.

The *Formula*, as we would expect, makes a clear distinction between forensic justification and internal regeneration. The first is external and perfect; the latter is internal and to be perfected in the age to come. Article III reads:

> We believe, therefore, teach and confess that this very thing is our righteousness before God, namely, that God remits to us our sins

of mere grace, without any respect of our works, going before, present, or following, or of our worthiness or merit. For he bestows and imputes to us the righteousness of the obedience of Christ: for the sake of that righteousness we are received by God into favor and accounted righteous.

We believe, also, teach, and confess that faith alone is the means and instrument whereby we lay hold on Christ the Savior, and so in Christ lay hold on that righteousness which is able to stand before the judgment of God; for that faith, for Christ's sake, is imputed to us for righteousness (Rom. 4:5).

In section V of this same article, regeneration and vivification are said to refer to the renewing of man "which is rightly distinguished from the justification of faith." Later on the following is stated:

We believe, teach, and confess that, although antecedent contrition and subsequent new obedience do not appertain to the article of justification before God, yet we are not to imagine any such justifying faith as can exist and abide with a purpose of evil, to wit: of sinning and acting contrary to conscience. But after that man is justified by faith, then that true and living faith works by love (Gal. 5:6), and good works always follow justifying faith, and are most certainly found together with it, provided only it be a true and living faith. For true faith is never alone, but hath always charity and hope in its train.

So while good works can have no place whatsoever in the justification of the believing sinner they are necessary, in the sense that they should arise from a free and spontaneous spirit of love for God and man.

The period immediately following the production of the *Formula* is often called the period of Lutheran orthodoxy, when the great dogmaticians produced their systematic theologies. Of such writers perhaps the best-known are Johann Gerhard (1582-1637) and J. A. Quenstedt (1617-1685), the last of the line being David Hollaz (1648-1713).[27] In their writings, justification is treated as external, forensic and imputed; further, it is clearly distinguished from sanctification and is thus presented as one among several important aspects of redemption/salvation. Though lip-service is paid to justification's being the article of faith by which the Church stands or falls, the doctrine does not hold the strategic place in their systems that it did in the teaching of Luther.

It is possible to claim, as does R. Preuss,[28] that Luther's teaching has not been changed in its content, only clarified in a new controversial situation. Following the controversy caused by Osiander's views as well as the teaching of the Council of Trent, it was simply not possible to continue to use the terminology of Luther, for if it had been used it would have played right into the hands of the enemy.

On the other hand, it is possible to claim that because of the preoccupation within Lutheran orthodoxy with the question of the *ordo salutis*, justification was actually made dependent upon repentance and faith within man. Certainly justification is carefully defined as an *actus Dei forensis in foro coeli* (a forensic act of God in the court of Heaven) in order to exclude anxious questionings of troubled consciences over the righteousness of their own works. However, in the *ordo salutis* justification is usually made to follow *vocatio* (calling), *illuminatio* (illumination), *regeneratio* (regeneration) and *conversio* (conversion). David Hollaz provides the following list: *De gratia vocante, illuminate, convertente, regenerante, justificante, inhabitante, renovante, conservante* and *glorificante*.

Thus, while justification is carefully defined as an act of God in Heaven and nondependent upon any spiritual/moral change in man, its place in the *ordo salutis* makes it dependent upon a change in man. What is gained by a radically objective definition of justification is apparently lost by its position in the order of God's producing salvation in and for man.

Luther, it will be recalled, held that justification is received in the form of faith since God justifies a sinner by giving him faith. Since man's will is enslaved, justification must be wholly and only the gift of grace.

7   The Council of Trent

In the bull *Laetare Jerusalem* (from Isa. 66:10), Pope Paul III called a Council of the Church into being; it met in Trent in northern Italy in 1545. Apart from dealing with the issues raised by the growth of Protestantism, it also intended to bring reform into the Roman Church and to advise on the menace created by the Ottoman Turks.[1]

The debates on justification within the Council followed the production of the decree on original sin. The bishops and theologians were conscious that their work on justification would be their most important theological production. Reporting to Rome on June 21, 1546 they wrote: "The significance of this Council in the theological sphere lies chiefly in the article on justification; in fact this is the most important item the Council has to deal with."[2] They began from positions which covered a wide spectrum of views, some of which were not too far from Luther's own position. Eventually they decided to produce their teaching around the model of the conversion of an unbeliever to the Christian faith. This is interesting and shows the desire to try to see the issue from the perspective of early Christianity. They divided the problems into: (1) How is a man justified? (God's action and man's response, the significance of faith); (2) How is progress in justification made?; and (3) In the event of the loss of grace, how is a person restored and justification renewed? After the rejection or improvement of various drafts, the final statement was enthusiastically passed at the beginning of the sixth session on January 13, 1547.

This Tridentine decree on justification is the Roman Catholic Church's answer to the teaching of Luther and the early Lutheran Confessions of Faith. Little if any notice was taken of Calvinist teaching. It served to make clear the basic differences between Roman Catholic dogma and Protestant teaching. The thirty-three canons expose and condemn errors while the sixteen chapters provide the positive teaching. The latter have a triple gradation (as the method of study required): 1—9, 10—13, and 14—16.[3]

The Positive Teaching

Chapters 1—9. Chapter 1, in recalling the earlier decree on original sin, declares that neither by man's natural powers nor by the moral law is he to be justified before God. In contrast, chapter 2 points to the incarnate Son, Jesus Christ, as the Savior of both Jew and Gentile.

Chapter 3 affirms that those to whom the merit of the passion of Christ is communicated are justified: "seeing that, in that new birth (John 3:3-6), there is bestowed upon them, through the merit of his passion, the grace whereby they are made just." Justification means to be *made*, not declared, just or righteous.

In chapter 4 justification is defined as being "a translation, from that state wherein man is born a child of Adam, to the state of grace, and of the adoption of the sons of God, through the second Adam, Jesus Christ, our Savior. And this translation, since the promulgation of the gospel, cannot be effected, without the laver of regeneration. . . ." Justification is a process which begins with the event of baptism, the "laver of regeneration."

Chapter 5 explains the necessity of preparation for justification in adults. By the illumination of the Spirit the heart of man is turned towards God, but man must respond positively and cooperate with the leading of the Spirit. "He is not able by his own free will, without the grace of God, to move himself unto justice in his sight."

More information on preparation for justification (which includes regeneration) is provided in chapter 6. Prompted and assisted by the Holy Spirit, sinners believe God's revealed promises of salvation and turn towards the Lord, knowing that he is the God of mercy; "and they begin to love him as the fountain of all justice; and are therefore moved against sins by a certain hatred and detestation, to wit, by that penitence which must be performed before baptism, to begin a new life and to keep the commandments of God."

Chapter 7 is one of the more important chapters and begins by defining justification as "not remission of sins merely, but also the sanctification and renewal of the inward man, through the voluntary reception of the grace, and the gifts, whereby man of unjust becomes just, and of an enemy a friend, so that he may be an heir according to hope of life everlasting."

Then, in medieval style, the causes of justification—final, efficient, meritorious, instrumental and formal—are explained.

Of this justification the causes are these: the *final* cause indeed is the glory of God and of Jesus Christ, and life everlasting; while the *efficient* cause is a merciful God who washes and sanctifies

gratuitously, signing, and anointing with the Holy Spirit of promise, who is the pledge of our inheritance; but the *meritorious*
cause is his most beloved only-begotten, our Lord Jesus Christ,
who, when we were enemies, for the exceeding charity wherewith he loved us, merited justification for us by his most holy
Passion on the wood of the cross, and made satisfaction for us
unto God the Father; the *instrumental* cause is the sacrament of
baptism, which is the sacrament of faith, without which (faith) no
man was ever justified; lastly, the alone *formal* cause is the justice
of God, not that whereby he himself is just, but that whereby he
maketh us just, that, to wit, with which we, being endowed by
him, are renewed in the spirit of our mind, and we are not only
reputed, but are truly called, and are just, receiving justice within
us, each one according to his own measure, which the Holy
Ghost distributes to every one as he wills, and according to each
one's proper disposition and cooperation. For although no one
can be just, but he to whom the merits of the Passion of our Lord
Jesus Christ are communicated, yet is this done in the said justification of the impious, when by the merit of that same most holy
Passion, the charity of God is poured forth, by the Holy Spirit, in
the hearts of those that are justified, and is inherent therein:
whence, man through Jesus Christ, in whom he is ingrafted,
receives, in the said justification, together with the remission of
sins, all these (gifts) infused at once, faith, hope, and charity. For
faith, unless hope and charity be added thereto, neither unites
man perfectly with Christ, nor makes him a living member of his
body.

Here is the heart of the Tridentine doctrine. The formal cause is
imparted and inherent righteousness, while true faith is always accompanied by hope and charity.

Chapter 8 acknowledges the primacy of faith and states that "faith
is the beginning of human salvation, the foundation, and the root of all
justification." Yet faith does not merit salvation. It merely precedes
justification. A polemical strain enters in chapter 9 which is "against
the vain confidence of heretics." This confidence (of Protestants) is the
assurance of justification which they claim to enjoy within their souls.
In contrast, the received Catholic theology teaches that "for even as no
pious person ought to doubt of the mercy of God, of the merit of
Christ, and of the virtue and efficacy of the sacraments, even so each
one, when he regards himself and his own weakness and indisposition,
may have fear and apprehension touching his own grace; seeing that no
one can know with a certainty of faith, which cannot be subject to error,
that he has obtained the grace of God."

Chapters 10—13. Justification, states chapter 10, is the process
of becoming just and is thus to be increased within the faithful. "They,
through the observance of the commandments of God and of the

Church, faith cooperating with good works, increase in that justice which they have received through the grace of Christ, and are still further justified." The need to keep God's commandments continually is emphasized in chapter 11. "Whoso are the sons of God love Christ; but they who love him keep his commandments . . . which assuredly with the divine help they can do." Those who persist will never be forsaken by God, "for God forsakes not those who have been once justified by his grace, unless he be first forsaken by them." It is a rash presumption, however, as chapter 12 declares, for a Christian to presume that he is surely one of the elect. In fact, as chapter 13 makes clear, perseverance is a gift of God; so "let those who think themselves to stand, take heed lest they fall, and, with fear and trembling work out their salvation in labors, in watchings, in almsdeeds, in prayers and oblations, in fastings and chastity. . . ."

Chapters 14—16. Chapter 14 is concerned with the recovery of the state of justification through the sacrament of penance by those who have fallen from grace. In the following chapter it is claimed that "the received grace of justification is lost, not only by infidelity whereby even faith itself is lost, but also by any other mortal sin whatever, though faith be not lost." The distinction between mortal (or deadly or grave) and venial sin is common in Roman Catholic theology. While the former deprives the Christian of sanctifying grace, the latter does not. Venial sins have been called "daily sins" or "light sins." The purpose of the sacrament of penance is to forgive sins committed after baptism and to restore the penitent to the position obtained at baptism.

In the final chapter (16) the merit of good works is described. "Life eternal is to be proposed to those working well unto the end and hoping in God, both as a grace mercifully promised to the sons of God through Jesus Christ, and as a reward which is according to the promise of God himself, to be faithfully rendered to their good works and merits." It continues:

> For, whereas Jesus Christ himself continually infuses his virtue into the said justified, as the head into the members, and the vine into the branches, and this virtue always precedes and accompanies and follows their good works, which without it could not in any wise be pleasing and meritorious before God, we must believe that nothing further is wanting to the justified, to prevent their being accounted to have, by those very works which have been done in God, fully satisfied the divine law according to the state of this life, and to have truly merited eternal life, to be obtained also in its (due) time, if so be, however, that they depart in grace.

Explaining the nature of infused and inherent righteousness (justice) the chapter states: "Neither is our own justice established as our own from ourselves; nor is the justice of God ignored or repudiated: for that justice which is called ours, because that we are justified from its being inherent in us, that same is (the justice) of God, because that it is infused into us of God, through the merit of Christ."

It will perhaps be helpful to summarize the main features of the Roman doctrine of justification.

1. Justification is both an event and a process. An unrighteous man becomes a righteous man. Becoming a child of God in baptism and having the remission of sins, the Christian is made righteous. If in the process he loses faith or falls away, he is restored through the sacrament of penance.

2. Justification occurs because of the infusion of the grace of God into the soul whereby inherent righteousness becomes a quality of the soul.

3. This imparted, infused and inherent righteousness is the formal cause of justification, while the meritorious cause is the passion of Christ.

4. Only at the end of the process will the believer truly know that he is justified. His constant duty is to cooperate with the grace of God given to him.

While it is true that the decree of the Council of Trent established Roman doctrine and excluded certain debates, it is not true that Trent actually prohibited all further exploration of the theme. But the exploration has been over secondary aspects of the doctrine, not over the central tenets—e.g., over what precisely cooperation with the prevenient grace of God really means. Had this teaching been the official and general teaching of the Church in 1517, perhaps Luther would never have felt the need to set forth his own understanding of the righteousness which is by faith. Adolf von Harnack has written that "the decree on justification, though an artificial product, is in many respects an excellent piece of work; in fact one may doubt whether the Reformation would have developed if this decree had been issued by the Lateran Council at the opening of the century and had really passed into the Church's flesh and blood."[4]

Canons, Errors and Heresies

Jedin provides the following helpful explanation concerning the relation of the chapters to the canons:

The Council's aim was to draw a line of demarcation between Catholic dogma and belief and Protestant teaching. This delimitating function of the decree was realized, in the first instance, by means of thirty-three canons which are no mere appendage of the doctrinal chapters. As a matter of fact the doctrinal chapters explain the canons; they are the positive formulation of the content of the faith which underlies the condemnation of the errors listed in the canons. On the other hand, in accordance with the whole purpose of the Council, the canons are of decisive importance. It is therefore a safe rule for an interpretation of the decree that it must always start from this delimiting function—that is, from the canons.[5]

Thus to the canons we turn.

It must be quickly emphasized that the canons are not aimed at Protestant teaching as the Protestants themselves would have expressed it and did express it. The majority of the canons are aimed at that understanding of Lutheran teaching found within the Roman Catholic Church. We know from much experience that what is said by one side is not always strictly identical with what is heard and understood on the other. For example, these two canons show how Lutheran doctrine was heard:

> *Canon XIII:* If any one saith, that it is necessary for every one, for the obtaining the remission of sins, that he believe for certain, and without any wavering arising from his own infirmity and indisposition, that his sins are forgiven him: let him be anathema.

> *Canon XV:* If any one saith, that a man, born again and justified, is bound of faith to believe that he is assuredly in the number of the predestinate: let him be anathema.

In fact, it is difficult to find one canon which anathematizes teaching which is presented in such a way as to be acceptable to Lutherans as a fair statement of their confession of faith. Some come very near to being fair accounts of Luther's position. For example, Luther had a very strong view of the bondage of the human will and this is noted in Canon IV.

> If any one saith, that man's free-will moved and excited by God, by assenting to God exciting and calling, nowise cooperates towards disposing and preparing itself for obtaining the grace of justification; that it can not refuse its consent, if it would, but that as something inanimate, it does nothing whatever and is merely passive: let him be anathema.

Further Luther emphasized over and over again that justification is by faith—that is, wholehearted trust in the God of mercy and grace. Canons XI and XII state:

> *Canon XI:* If any one saith, that men are justified, either by the sole imputation of the justice of Christ, or by the sole remission of sins, to the exclusion of the grace and charity which is poured forth in their hearts by the Holy Ghost, and is inherent in them; or even that the grace, whereby we are justified, is only the favor of God: let him be anathema.

Canon XII: If any one saith, that justifying faith is nothing else but confidence in the divine mercy which remits sins for Christ's sake; or, that this confidence alone is that whereby we are justified: let him be anathema.

In each case Luther's position is presented in such a way as not to do justice to his full teaching.

A few of the canons are aimed at old-fashioned Pelagian teaching which both Roman Catholics and Protestants condemned:

Canon I: If any one saith, that man may be justified before God by his own works, whether done through the teaching of human nature, or that of the law, without the grace of God through Jesus Christ: let him be anathema.

Canon II: If any one saith, that the grace of God, through Jesus Christ, is given only for this, that man may be able more easily to live justly and to merit eternal life, as if, by free-will without grace, he were able to do both, though hardly indeed and with difficulty: let him be anathema.

Canon III: If any one saith, that without the prevenient inspiration of the Holy Ghost, and without his help, man can believe, hope, love, or be penitent as he ought, so that the grace of justification may be bestowed upon him: let him be anathema.

Here, at least, there was agreement.

From two leading Protestant theologians came replies to the dogma of the Council of Trent. John Calvin, the Genevan reformer, produced *Acta Synodi Tridentini cum Antidoto* and Martin Chemnitz, the Lutheran theologian, wrote *Examen Concilii Tridentii.* Chemnitz was well aware that there was a disagreement over what *dikaioun* means. Is it the same as *justificare?*

The papalists simply argue that the word justify properly signifies a movement, a change, from unrighteousness to righteousness, as when in natural movements one quality is driven out and another is brought in. For they want to treat the composition of the word "justify" *(justificare)* according to the analogy of the words *sanctificare* ("to make holy"), *vivificare* ("to make alive"), *calefacerex* ("to make warm"), *frigefacerex* ("to make cold"), etc.[6]

The papalists are wrong. The Greek verb *dikaioun* has a forensic meaning of, "to declare righteous."

Further, Chemnitz pinpointed the central issue as relating to the formal cause: Is it God's work in us or God's work outside us?

It is regarding the good works of the regenerate, or the new obedience, that there is now the chief controversy between the papalists and us, namely, whether the regenerate are justified by that newness which the Holy Spirit works in them and by the good works which follow from that renewal; that is, whether the newness, the virtues, or good works of the regenerate are the things by which they can stand in the judgment of God that they may not be condemned, on account of which they have a gracious and propitiated God, to which they should look, on which they should rely, in which they should trust when they are dealing with that difficult question, how we may be children of God and be accepted to eternal life.[7]

While insisting that the regenerate do produce the fruit of righteousness by the help of the indwelling Spirit, Chemnitz insisted that the indwelling righteousness of God's work in us is not the formal cause of justification. It is the mediatorial righteousness of Christ by which we are justified.

What was not explicitly stated at Trent and what was never therefore seriously discussed in the sixteenth century is the later Roman Catholic understanding of justification as a making righteous arising from the effectual declaratory word of the Lord by which a sinner is declared righteous. This understanding was explained by Cardinal John Henry Newman in 1837 and has been restated by both Hans Küng and Michael Schmaus. We shall note this when we discuss Roman Catholic theology in a later chapter.

8 The Reformed View

Of all the early teachers of those Protestant Churches which are now Reformed in name or tradition, John Calvin stands supreme. It is to his doctrine that we now turn.

John Calvin (1509-1564)[1]

After a humanist training in the classics and law, Calvin experienced a change of direction in his life as he adopted the basic Lutheran insights concerning the gospel of Jesus Christ. As Luther had sought for a gracious God, so Calvin, turning away from the corruptions of the Roman Catholic Church, began to search for a pure church. French by birth, he became the chief pastor and reformer of Geneva, a small French-speaking republic in Switzerland. Under his influence the city became a great center of theological study, Bible translation and reforming activity.

By all accounts he was a remarkable, if austere, man. His theological insights, his great ability as an exegete and commentator on the Bible, his linguistic ability in Hebrew, Greek, Latin and French, his precision of mind, his clear and pithy style and his total dedication to duty made him the most influential writer among all the Reformers. For his doctrines of justification and sanctification, the most obvious as well as the best place to look is his *Institutes of the Christian Religion,* which first appeared in Latin in 1535 and reached its final edition in 1559.[2] In Book Three, "The way in which we receive the grace of Christ: what benefits come to us from it, and what effects follow," we find his teaching on justification. It is easy to read and clear in its contents. Many people have found that to read Calvin is actually easier than to read accounts of his teaching.

Before looking at the teaching of the *Institutes,* it is helpful to note the *Confession of Faith* (1536) which was, if not written by, at least approved by Calvin. This *Confession* was intended to serve as a basis of faith for all the citizens of Geneva.[3] Sections 6—8 are as follows:

6. SALVATION IN JESUS

We confess then that it is Jesus Christ who is given to us by the Father, in order that in him we should recover all of which in ourselves we are deficient. Now all that Jesus Christ has done and suffered for our redemption, we veritably hold without any doubt, as it is contained in the Creed, which is recited in the Church, that is to say: I believe in God the Father Almighty, and so on.

7. RIGHTEOUSNESS IN JESUS

Therefore we acknowledge the things which are consequently given to us by God in Jesus Christ: first, that being in our own natures enemies of God and subjects of his wrath and judgment, we are reconciled with him and received again in grace through the intercession of Jesus Christ, so that by his righteousness and guiltlessness we have remission of our sins, and by the shedding of his blood we are cleansed and purified from all our stains.

8. REGENERATION IN JESUS

Second, we acknowledge that by his Spirit we are regenerated into a new spiritual nature. That is to say that the evil desires of our flesh are mortified by grace, so that they rule us no longer. On the contrary, our will is rendered conformable to God's will, to follow in his way and to seek what is pleasing to him. Therefore we are by him delivered from the servitude of sin, under whose power we were of ourselves held captive, and by this deliverance we are made capable and able to do good works and not otherwise.

This is reasonably simple and straightforward. However, in the light of what we shall note in the teaching of Calvin two points are worth making. First, the order followed here is justification and then regeneration/sanctification, which is the way Melanchthon had begun to teach within Lutheranism.[4] Secondly, the reference to "the intercession of Jesus Christ" is a theme which constantly appears in the *Institutes* in the discussion of justification.

Having set the scene, we shall now look at the teaching of Calvin as it is found in the *Institutes* and summarize it under seven headings.

1. Spiritual union with Christ is the way God the Father gives salvation to his elect. God's work of reconciliation was not completed at Easter or on Ascension Day. It continued in the work of the Holy Spirit bringing Christ to the elect and the elect to Christ.[5] "We must understand that as long as Christ remains outside of us and we are separated from him, all that he has suffered and done for the salvation of the human race remains useless and of no value to us" (3:1:1). And, "All that he possesses is nothing to us until we grow into one body with him" (3:1:1). By spiritual union or communion with Christ, Calvin was not thinking of the absorption of the human personality into Christ. The teaching of Andreas Osiander of Königsberg, which included certain mystical speculations concerning union with Christ, caused Calvin to be more careful in the way he expressed his own understanding of spiritual union. He emphasized that communion with Christ was in and by the Holy Spirit alone, the Spirit who may be called the Spirit of Christ because he bears the name and characteristics of Christ. "Christ unites himself to us by the Spirit alone. By the grace and power of the same Spirit we are made his members, to keep us under himself and in turn to possess him" (3:1:3).

2. Faith is a gift of God and the principal work of the Holy Spirit in the elect. Calvin held that "faith is the principal work of the Holy Spirit" and defined faith in this way: "a firm and certain knowledge of God's benevolence towards us, founded upon the truth of the freely given promise in Christ, both revealed to our minds and sealed upon our hearts through the Holy Spirit" (3:2:7). True faith originates in the secret work of the Holy Spirit in the human heart. It knows and rests upon God's gracious promises of salvation given in the gospel, and it includes the assurance of God's love. The Holy Spirit actually works in perfect harmony with the Word of God. This means that faith is created either by the Holy Spirit, or by the Word of God in Scripture (and as preached) or by Word and Spirit together. The mind absorbs the Word of God, which then enters the heart. "For the Word of God is not received by faith if it flits about in the top of the brain, but when it takes root in the depth of the heart that it may be an invincible defense to withstand and drive off all the stratagems of temptation" (3:2:36).

By faith the elect receive Christ. "By partaking of him, we principally receive a double grace: namely, that being reconciled to God through Christ's blamelessness, we may have in Heaven instead of a judge a gracious Father; and secondly, that sanctified by Christ's spirit we may cultivate blamelessness and purity of life" (3:11:1). Faith is merely an "instrument," but rightly understood it is the only instrument by which the elect receive the grace of God.[6]

3. Faith possesses Christ and enjoys, as the effects of this union, repentance and forgiveness of sins. Calvin placed great emphasis on genuine repentance (or conversion) as a continuing process of growth in grace. How he saw it in relation to forgiveness and justification is made clear when he writes: "Now, both repentance and forgiveness of sins—that is, newness of life and reconciliation—are conferred on us by Christ, and both are attained by us through faith. As a consequence, reason and the order of teaching demand that I begin to discuss both at this point [i.e., Book 3:3:1]. However, our immediate transition will be from faith to repentance. For when this topic is rightly understood, it will better appear how man is justified by faith alone, and simple pardon; nevertheless actual holiness of life, so to speak, is not separated from free imputation of righteousness." Thus Calvin's method is to deal first with repentance (which includes regeneration and sanctification) and then turn to justification. By adopting such a method he was able to insist that true faith issues in holiness of life, as well as being the instrumental cause of a saving relationship with God.

4. *Repentance not only follows faith but is born of faith.* Calvin defined repentance or conversion as "the true turning of our life to God, a turning that arises from a pure and earnest fear of him; and it consists in the mortification of our flesh and of the old man, and in the vivification of the Spirit" (3:3:5). "Pure and earnest fear" of God arises from the knowledge that God is just, that I have grievously sinned against him and that I rightly deserve his punishment. So even when I approach God in Jesus Christ I know that what I receive by pure grace is not what I truly deserve.

Such fear is necessarily associated with mortification. This is the process initiated and helped on by the Spirit of Christ as he uses the "sword of the Spirit," which is the Word of God. It includes ceasing to do evil, overcoming the sinful bias within human nature, renouncing the world, the flesh and the devil, casting off the "old man," the continuous activity of self-denial and "taking up one's cross." Such fear is also associated with vivification, which occurs as mortification proceeds. This is the positive side and includes participating in the resurrection of Christ, putting on the new man, walking in the Spirit and being renewed according to the pattern of the image of God revealed in Christ.

Mortification and vivification are two sides of one coin. One can only truly occur in company with the other. Each depends on the other, and both are what "a true turning to God" implies. However, it has to be recognized that "this restoration does not take place in one moment or one day or one year; but through continual and sometimes slow advances God wipes out in his elect the corruptions of the flesh, cleanses them of guilt, consecrates them to himself as temples, renewing all their minds to true purity that they may practice repentance throughout their lives and know that this warfare will end only at death" (3:3:9). Believers never achieve sinless perfection in this life, for while sin has lost its dominion in their lives it still dwells in them, ever ready to assert itself. While Calvin taught that true repentance occurs in a child of God who fully participates in the life, worship and sacraments of the Church, he rejected the medieval and Roman doctrines of penance and auricular confession of sins.

5. *Faith receives and embraces the righteousness of God offered in the gospel and imputed to believers who are in union with Christ.* "Christ was given to us by God's generosity, to be grasped and possessed by us in faith" (3:11:1). Justification, wrote Calvin, is to be explained "simply as the acceptance with which God receives us into his favor as

righteous men. And we say that it consists in the remission of sins and the imputation of Christ's righteousness" (3:11:2). It is Christ in his work as high priest who is the One by whose presence and intercession in Heaven we are justified. United to him by the Spirit in faith, God the Father counts his righteousness as ours, so that we are justified because of his obedience to God as our substitute when he was on earth. Calvin held that we must lift up our minds to God's judgment-seat so we may be firmly convinced of his free justification. That he understood justification in a forensic manner is clear. However, it is not his primary emphasis since the forensic metaphor is dependent on the spiritual union with Christ and on the reality of the heavenly intercession of Christ, the high priest. "You see that our righteousness is not in us but in Christ, that we possess it only because we are partakers in Christ; indeed, in him we possess all its riches" (3:11:23).

Though Calvin refers to justification as the principal article of the Christian religion, he does not, like Luther, make it the central thrust of his whole theology and ethics. In fact, it is difficult to find one center to the theology of Calvin. Like Melanchthon (from whom he probably received the idea of forensic justification), Calvin was prepared to use some scholastic terminology in order to clarify his meaning. So he summarized his position in this way: "The efficient cause of our salvation consists in God the Father's love; the material cause in God the Son's obedience; the instrumental cause in the Spirit's illumination, that is, faith; the final cause, in the glory of God's great generosity" (3:14:21). Thus justification is by grace alone and by faith alone. We are justified by an alien righteousness and not, as the Council of Trent taught, by an imparted and inherent righteousness. Further, this alien righteousness is provided by the Son of God through what he achieved as our substitute in his human nature. The righteousness of Christ imputed to us is not, as Osiander taught, his eternal righteousness as eternal Son, but his mediatorial righteousness as incarnate Son and Messiah.

6. *The good works of true believers are acceptable to God through Christ.* Calvin utterly rejected good works as the basis for acceptance in God's heavenly court. This rejection related to good works before and after conversion. The reason is simple—only the mediatorial righteousness of Christ is acceptable to the Father. However, Calvin had to face the fact that both the Old and New Testaments imply that God accepts the good works of his children, even though his children are not yet perfected. As one of the greatest commentators in Holy Scripture, he accepted this fact and answered quite simply that the works are acceptable only because they are seen and received by God in the name of Jesus Christ. "Because the godly, encompassed with mortal flesh, are still sinners, and their good works are as yet incomplete and redolent of vices of the flesh, he can be propitious neither to the former nor to the latter unless he embrace them in Christ rather than in themselves. In this sense we are to understand those

passages which attest that God is kind and merciful to the keepers of righteousness" (3:17:5).

In a further explanation he wrote: "After forgiveness of sins is set forth, the good works that now follow are appraised otherwise than on their own merit. For everything imperfect in them is covered by Christ's perfection; every blemish or spot is cleansed away by his purity in order not to be brought in question at the divine judgment. Therefore, after the guilt of transgressions that hinder man from bringing forth anything pleasing to God has been blotted out, and after the fault of imperfection, which habitually defiles even good works, is buried, the good works done by believers are accounted righteous, or, what is the same thing are reckoned as righteous" (3:17:8).

Here is yet a further difference between Calvin and medieval (and Roman) theology. Calvin will only allow that works are good because of their acceptance by God in the name of Christ. Roman Catholic theology allows that since they proceed from imparted and inherent righteousness they are acceptable to God.

7. *Regeneration and forgiveness, sanctification and justification are inseparable in life, for both are blessings of union with Christ.* Already this point has been made. However, it is so important that it needs emphasizing. There is no justification in Heaven without regeneration on earth; there is no imputed righteousness in God's tribunal without accompanying good works in the arena of daily life. Responding to Osiander, Calvin wrote: "Yet we must bear in mind . . . that the grace of justification is not separated from regeneration, although they are things distinct. But because it is very well known by experience that the traces of sin always remain in the righteous, their justification must be very different from reformation into newness of life" (3:11:11). While a conceptual distinction may be made and, for clarity, must be made, in real life the two sides belong inseparably together if there is to be genuine Christianity.

After Calvin

Within the community of scholars who seek to understand and interpret the emergence and development of the Reformed faith (often called Calvinism), there is a difference of opinion as to the relationship of the teaching of Calvin to that of his "orthodox" successors. The two extremes of this spectrum of difference may be stated as: (1) the conviction that a serious distortion of Calvin's balanced insights especially occurred within federal theology with the result that (to use the theme of a book) *Calvin (is) Against the Calvinists;*[7] and (2) that Theodore Beza (1519-1605), Calvin's successor in Geneva, and later theologians merely developed Calvin's system in a logical way as they faced controversies and problems he did not have to face.[8]

This is not the place to discuss this question of difference of interpretation, but we must be aware of it as we notice the contents of certain Reformed Confessions of Faith, particular interests and insights of Reformed dogmaticians, and the influential Reformed theology taught at Princeton Seminary in the nineteenth century. We must also be aware of the fact that existing alongside the mainstream of Reformed orthodoxy have been those who, from within the Reformed Churches/tradition, have offered significantly different accounts of justification. Jacob Arminius (1560-1609) of the Netherlands, who gave his name to Arminianism, and Richard Baxter (1615-1691), the English Puritan whose theology was called Neonomianism by contemporaries, are famous examples.[9] Also, the hyper-Calvinists of the eighteenth century presented a theology which was heavily determined by the doctrine of the eternal decrees of God, and thus they spoke of the eternal justification and adoption of the elect before they were born.[10]

It is clear from a study of the Reformed tradition that there was agreement on the following beliefs: the *meritorious cause* of justification is the work of Christ as substitute of the elect; the *formal cause*, that by which God actually pronounces and accepts a sinner as righteous, is the righteousness of Christ, the mediator and high priest of the elect, who is in Heaven; and the *instrumental cause*, or the channel through which God actually achieved the justification of the sinner, is *faith* (faith that trusts God and expresses itself in faithfulness to him). The consciousness that the Roman Church had taken a very different position on justification and sanctification and the fact that its theologians strongly defended that different position meant that, as with Lutheran orthodoxy, Calvinist/Reformed orthodoxy expressed its beliefs in a controversial situation.

Reformed Confessions

There are many confessions of faith and catechisms produced by the Reformed Churches in the sixteenth and seventeenth centuries. Our attention will focus on only three—the *Belgic Confession,* the *Heidelberg Catechism* and the *Westminster Confession.*[11]

The *Belgic Confession* (1561) was produced for the Reformed Church in the Netherlands. Its author was Guido de Brès (Guy de Bray), who was executed on May 31, 1567. The Confession has thirty-seven articles. Article XX writes of God's justice and mercy: "God therefore manifested his justice against his Son when he laid our iniquities upon him, and poured forth his mercy and goodness on us, who were guilty and worthy of damnation, out of mere and perfect love, giving his Son unto death for us and raising him for our justification, that through him we might obtain immortality and life eternal." Article XXI describes the satisfaction presented by Christ on the cross to appease the wrath of God. Articles XXII—XXIV address our topic.

ART. XXII

Of Our Justification Through Faith in Jesus Christ

We believe that, to attain the true knowledge of this great mystery, the Holy Ghost kindleth in our hearts an upright faith, which embraces Jesus Christ with all his merits, appropriates

him, and seeks nothing more besides him. For it must needs
follow, either that all things which are requisite to our salvation
are not in Jesus Christ, or if all things are in him, that then those
who possess Jesus Christ through faith have complete salvation in
him. Therefore, for any to assert that Christ is not sufficient, but
that something more is required besides him, would be too gross
a blasphemy; for hence it would follow that Christ was but half a
Savior. Therefore we justly say with Paul, that "we are justified by
faith alone, or by faith without works." However, to speak more
clearly, we do not mean that faith itself justifies us, for it is only
an instrument with which we embrace Christ our Righteousness.
But Jesus Christ, imputing to us all his merits, and so many holy
works, which he hath done for us and in our stead, is our Righteousness. And faith is an instrument that keeps us in communion with him in all his benefits, which, when they become ours,
are more than sufficient to acquit us of our sins.

ART. XXIII

Our Justification Consists in the Forgiveness of Sin and the Imputation of Christ's Righteousness

We believe that our salvation consists in the remission of
our sins for Jesus Christ's sake, and that therein our righteousness
before God is implied; as David and Paul teach us, declaring this
to be the happiness of man, that God imputes righteousness to
him without works. And the same Apostle saith, that we are
justified freely by his grace, through the redemption which is in
Jesus Christ. And therefore we always hold fast this foundation,
ascribing all the glory to God, humbling ourselves before him,
and acknowledging ourselves to be such as we really are, without
presuming to trust in any thing in ourselves, or in any merit of
ours, relying and resting upon the obedience of Christ crucified
alone, which becomes ours when we believe in him. This is
sufficient to cover all our iniquities, and to give us confidence in
approaching to God; freeing the conscience of fear, terror, and
dread, without following the example of our first father, Adam,
who, trembling, attempted to cover himself with fig-leaves. 'And,
verily, if we should appear before God, relying on ourselves or on
any other creature, though ever so little, we should, alas! be
consumed. And therefore every one must pray with David: "O
Lord, enter not into judgment with thy servant: for in thy sight
shall no man living be justified."

ART. XXIV

Of Man's Sanctification and Good Works

We believe that this true faith, being wrought in man by the
hearing of the Word of God and the operation of the Holy Ghost,

doth regenerate and make him a new man, causing him to live a new life, and freeing him from the bondage of sin. Therefore it is so far from being true, that this justifying faith makes men remiss in a pious and holy life, that on the contrary without it they would never do anything out of love to God, but only out of self-love or fear of damnation. Therefore it is impossible that this holy faith can be unfruitful in man: for we do not speak of a vain faith, but of such a faith as is called in Scripture "a faith that worketh by love," which excites man to the practice of those works which God has commanded in his Word. Which works, as they proceed from the good root of faith, are good and acceptable in the sight of God, forasmuch as they are all sanctified by his grace: howbeit they are of no account towards our justification. For it is by faith in Christ that we are justified, even before we do good works, otherwise they could not be good works any more than the fruit of a tree can be good before the tree itself is good.

Therefore we do good works, but not to merit by them (for what can we merit?)—nay, we are beholden to God for the good works we do, and not he to us, "since it is he that worketh in us both to will and to do of his good pleasure." Let us therefore attend to what is written: "When ye shall have done all those things which are commanded you, say we are unprofitable servants: we have done that which was our duty to do."

In the meantime we do not deny that God rewards good works, but it is through his grace that he crowns his gifts. Moreover, though we do good works, we do not found our salvation upon them; for we can do no work but what is polluted by our flesh, and also punishable; and although we could perform such works, still the remembrance of one sin is sufficient to make God reject them. Thus, then, we should always be in doubt, tossed to and fro without any certainty, and our poor consciences would be continually vexed if they relied not on the merits of the suffering and death of our Savior.

Concerning whether or not the doctrine is identical with that of Calvin, the answer must be both positive and negative. Probably Calvin actually approved it when it was taken to Geneva to be shown to the pastors there. However, we may note some differences. First of all, justification is treated before sanctification and both follow the treatment of eternal election in Article XVI. Here is a difference at least in methodology and is more in agreement with the method of Beza than of Calvin. The latter discussed eternal election in the *Institutes* after justification. Then, secondly, there appears to be a more positive value given the worth of good works performed by the Christian in the Confession than in Calvin's treatment.

The *Heidelberg Catechism* derives its name from Heidelberg, the major city of the Palatinate in Germany. In 1562 the Elector, Frederic the Pious, directed that a catechism be prepared, and the task was given to Zacarias Ursinus, a professor of theology in the university. After being approved by the faculty of theology, it was introduced into the churches and schools in 1563. Soon afterwards it was translated into Dutch and so became an important doctrinal standard in both the German and Dutch Reformed Churches.

Q. 60. *How are you righteous before God?*
A. Only by true faith in Jesus Christ. In spite of the fact that my conscience accuses me that I have grievously sinned against all the commandments of God, and have not kept any one of them, and that I am still ever prone to all that is evil, nevertheless, God, without any merit of my own, out of pure grace, grants me the benefits of the perfect expiation of Christ, imputing to me his righteousness and holiness as if I had never committed a single sin or had ever been sinful, having fulfilled myself all the obedience which Christ has carried out for me, if only I accept such favor with a trusting heart.

Q. 61. *Why do you say that you are righteous by faith alone?*
A. Not because I please God by virtue of the worthiness of my faith, but because the satisfaction, righteousness, and holiness of Christ alone are my righteousness before God, and because I can accept it and make it mine in no other way than by faith alone.

Q. 62. *But why cannot our good works be our righteousness before God, or at least a part of it?*
A. Because the righteousness which can stand before the judgment of God must be absolutely perfect and wholly in conformity with the divine Law. But even our best works in this life are all imperfect and defiled with sin.

Q. 63. *Will our good works merit nothing, even when it is God's purpose to reward them in this life, and in the future life as well?*
A. This reward is not given because of merit, but out of grace.

Q. 64. *But does not this teaching make people careless and sinful?*
A. No, for it is impossible for those who are ingrafted into Christ by true faith not to bring forth the fruit of gratitude.

It is interesting to observe that the questions on justification and good works occur in the general section headed "The Holy Spirit" (for Lord's Day 20—24). The first answer (53) in this section describes the role of the Spirit in regeneration and in the creation of true faith. Apart from this, the Catechism has no discussion of sanctification and likewise no discussion of election.

Finally we turn to Britain for the *Westminster Confession of Faith* (1647). This was produced by divines of the Church of England who wished to "purify" the Church in a Reformed direction and visited Scottish divines from the Reformed Church of Scotland. Though produced in England, it was never adopted by the Church of England but has become the basic confession of the English-speaking Presbyterian Churches whose roots are associated with the Church of Scotland, which adopted it in 1648.

The Confession reflects a federal theology and speaks of a covenant of works that God made with Adam and a covenant of grace made between members of the Holy Trinity in order to bring salvation to the elect. It has a very strong emphasis on predestination and the decrees of God; all that is affirmed concerning the work of Christ, the gift of salvation and the Church is written in the light of this emphasis.

Chapter X, entitled "Effectual Calling," explains how all those who are predestinated unto life are called by the Word and Spirit out of sin into the grace of God. Chapter XI is on justification, XII on adoption and XIII on sanctification.

Justification

1. Those whom God effectually calleth, he also freely justifieth: not by infusing righteousness into them, but by pardoning their sins, and by accounting and accepting their persons as righteous; not for any thing wrought in them, or done by them, but for Christ's sake alone; not by imputing faith itself, the act of believing, or any other evangelical obedience to them, as their righteousness, but by imputing the obedience and satisfaction of Christ unto them, they receiving and resting on him and his righteousness by faith; which faith they have not of themselves: it is the gift of God.

2. Faith, thus receiving and resting on Christ and his righteousness, is the alone instrument of justification; yet is it not alone in the person justified, but is ever accompanied with all other saving graces, and is no dead faith, but worketh by love.

3. Christ, by his obedience and death, did fully discharge the debt of all those that are thus justified, and did make a proper, real, and full satisfaction to his Father's justice in their behalf. Yet, inasmuch as he was given by the Father for them, and his obedience and satisfaction accepted in their stead, and both freely, not for any thing in them, their justification is only of free grace; that both the exact justice and rich grace of God might be glorified in the justification of sinners.

4. God did, from all eternity, decree to justify all the elect; and Christ did, in the fullness of time, die for their sins, and rise again for their justification; nevertheless they are not justified until the Holy Spirit doth, in due time, actually apply Christ unto them.

5. God doth continue to forgive the sins of those that are justified: and, although they can never fall from the state of justification, yet they may by their sins fall under God's fatherly displeasure, and not have the light of his countenance restored unto them until they humble themselves, confess their sins, beg pardon, and renew their faith and repentance.

6. The justification of believers under the Old Testament was, in all these respects, one and the same with the justification of believers under the New Testament.

Of Adoption

1. All those that are justified, God vouchsafeth, in and for his only Son, Jesus Christ, to make partakers of the grace of adoption: by which they are taken into the number, and enjoy the liberties and privileges of the children of God; have his name put upon them; receive the Spirit of adoption; have access to the throne of grace with boldness; are enabled to cry Abba, Father; are pitied, protected, provided for, and chastened by him as by a father; yet never cast off, but sealed to the day of redemption, and inherit the promises, as heirs of everlasting salvation.

Of Sanctification

1. They who are effectually called and regenerated, having a new heart and a new spirit created in them, are further sanctified, really and personally, through the virtue of Christ's death and resurrection, by his Word and Spirit dwelling in them: the dominion of the whole body of sin is destroyed, and the several lusts thereof are more and more weakened and mortified; and they more and more quickened and strengthened, in all saving graces, to the practice of true holiness, without which no man shall see the Lord.

2. This sanctification is throughout in the whole man, yet imperfect in this life: there abideth still some remnants of corruption in every part, whence ariseth a continual and irreconcilable war, the flesh lusting against the Spirit, and the Spirit against the flesh.

3. In which war, although the remaining corruption for a time may much prevail, yet, through the continual supply of strength from the sanctifying Spirit of Christ, the regenerate part doth overcome: and so the saints grow in grace, perfecting holiness in the fear of God.

The next three chapters look at saving faith, repentance unto life and good works. In that God looks upon the believer "in his Son, he is pleased to accept and reward what is sincere, although accompanied with many weaknesses and imperfections."

The difference between the teaching of Calvin and the *Confession* lies in the areas of methodology and of emphasis. The structural importance of federal theology, together with the fact that the doctrines of the eternal decrees and of limited atonement are placed before the discussion of calling, justification and sanctification, serve to give these latter doctrines a different flavor. This is seen in the *ordo salutis*. In Calvin's teaching it is union with Christ-faith-regeneration (justification)/repentance/sanctification-glorification. In the Westminster theology, it is effectual calling-regeneration-saving faith-justification-adoption-sanctification. Further, while true faith in Calvin's teaching is primarily personal knowledge of God as Savior and includes assurance of salvation and precedes repentance, in Westminster theology faith follows repentance and does not contain an assurance of salvation.[12] Whether or not we are dealing with a distortion of Calvin's original insights, or whether we are seeing the logical and systematic outworking in different circumstances of his teaching is difficult to judge.

The concerns of the continental Reformed theologians (or Reformed dogmaticians/scholastic Calvinist divines) were much the same as those who gathered in Westminster Abbey, London. They differ from Calvin both in their methodology and emphases. They went in for precise logical distinctions and definitions (as did the Lutheran divines) as they sought to provide coherent theological systems and defend them against attack.[13] The effect of such logical procedures was to drive a wedge between justification and sanctification in order to clearly distinguish imputed from inherent righteousness. Another wedge that was used was to separate Christ from his merits, to think of Christ as shedding his merits and leaving them in the heavenly court so they could be used for forensic justification. For example, Johannes Wollebius (1586-1629), professor in Basel, wrote in his *Compendium Theologiae Christianae* (1626) that "the expression 'We are justified by faith' is a metonymy and has the same meaning as 'We are justified by the merit of Christ which is apprehended by faith' " (chap. 30). Such teaching constantly had to face the charge of "legal fiction" by those who felt that justification was being removed from the area of real Christian experience.

In part this charge was met by making a distinction between active and passive justification, and also in part by careful explanations of what *forensic* really meant. Heppe claims that "the distinction between 'active' and 'passive' justification is immovably fixed in Reformed dogmatics."[14] Active justification is the actual execution (from the believer's perspective in space-time) of the eternal decree of justification in which the believing sinner is absolved and declared righteous. Passive justification is the later knowledge within the soul of the believer that he is in fact truly justified in Heaven. It is related to the witness of the Spirit and the experience of the fruit of the Spirit. It is also related to the daily experience of the forgiveness of sins which are confessed to God.

The Nineteenth Century
The story of Reformed theology from the seventeenth to the nineteenth centuries is not particularly fascinating in terms of the exposition of the doctrines of salvation. Traditional orthodoxy survived and possibly hardened its sinews as it responded to the Enlightenment. The birth of foreign missions at the end of the eighteenth century also had its effect,

making those holding orthodox views ask how their doctrine related to the practice of evangelism.

In the nineteenth century there was within the Presbyterian Churches of Scotland and North America a significant school of thought which expressed a powerful allegiance to the theology of the Westminster Confession of Faith. Princeton Seminary in the north and Columbia Seminary in the south of the USA, along with New College (under the control of the Free Church of Scotland) in Edinburgh, were important academic centers where Westminster Orthodoxy (or federal theology/high Calvinism) was expounded with great clarity in the context of the intellectual climate of the day. In his *Systematic Theology* (three volumes, 1872, 1873) Charles Hodge (1797-1878) expounded the doctrines of justification and sanctification as found in the *Westminster Confession* and the *Catechisms,* making use of the famous exposition of Jonathan Edwards (1703-1758), America's greatest philosopher-theologian, and also of the treatise of John Owen (1616-1683), the great English Congregationalist divine.[15] In particular, he opposed Arminian and Romanist doctrines as he explained Reformed orthodoxy. His son, Archibald A. Hodge (1823-1886) succeeded his father at Princeton in 1877. His exposition of the *Westminster Confession of Faith,* known as *The Confession of Faith* (1869), had already been published. In this, his exposition of justification and sanctification is exceedingly clear. Neither father nor son had any intention of deviating from the orthodoxy of the received *Confession.* The only differences which can be detected are the following: (1) there is a heightening of the background of federal theology in the Princeton school, as (2) there is also, by the use of the Scottish common-sense philosophy, a supreme confidence that the Princeton doctrine is true and accords with genuine Christian experience.[16]

In Scotland a professor of theology in New College, Edinburgh published his lectures on justification. James Buchanan's *The Doctrine of Justification: An Outline of Its History in the Church and of Its Exposition from Scripture* (1867, reprinted 1961) appeared partly as a response to the controversy over the doctrine of justification which had occurred in the Church of England earlier that century. His aim was to show that the received Reformed doctrine was both taught in Scripture and recognized by the worthiest of divines over the centuries. To achieve this aim, he had to show the errors of other viewpoints—Arminian, Socinian, Antinomian, Roman, etc.—and to make certain claims that few today would uphold (e.g., that the doctrine of forensic imputation was taught in the Church before the sixteenth century).

While it is the case that many of the theologians within the old Reformed and Presbyterian denominations have felt the need to question the biblical basis of the received Reformed orthodoxy, it is also true that there remain large numbers in these denominations, and especially in the newer Reformed denominations, who confidently believe that the received orthodoxy is wholly in accord with Scripture and needs no reexamination.

9   The Anglican Approach

The Church of England experienced "a washing of her dirty face" in the sixteenth century. At least this is how many of those sympathetic to the cause of Protestant reform described what happened to the national Church. While preserving her episcopate and many of her traditional structures, she gained the monarch as her "supreme governor," her own English liturgy and canon law, with a new Protestant Confession of Faith. The Church of England received ideas from Lutheran Germany and from the Reformed Churches and adapted them to English conditions. In these years of change (1529-1559) the national Church produced no great theologian to stand alongside Luther or Calvin; but in the person of her Archbishop, Thomas Cranmer, she had a wise and sober leader. He was chiefly responsible for the adaptation of those continental ideas which found their way into the doctrine and liturgy of the Elizabethan Settlement of Religion.

Thomas Cranmer (1489-1556)[1]
Cranmer's doctrine of justification began and continued under the influence of Luther and Melanchthon, especially the latter. In the discussions between English and Lutheran theologians in 1538 Cranmer was happy with their agreed statement on justification:

> Sinners . . . are justified not because of the worthiness or merit of their repentance or of any works or of their own merits, but freely for Christ's sake through faith when they believe that they are received into grace and that their sins are forgiven for Christ's sake, who by his death made satisfaction for our sins. God regards this faith as righteousness in his sight, Romans 3 & 4.

This is article 4 of the document known as *The Thirteen Articles*, a statement which Henry VIII never accepted as binding on the Church of England.[2]

A few years later Cranmer was busy composing a sermon on justification, to be part of a collection of homilies to be read in parish churches. In fact it was not published until 1547, when young Edward VI was king. It is probable that Cranmer revised his original draft before the publication of the *Homilies*. Cranmer's homily came to have special doctrinal importance, as the later *Articles of Religion* referred to it for an authoritative exposition of justification. In the light of this, it will be best to look at the *Articles* and then at the *Homily.*

There are two sets of *Articles* to examine. The first, for whose preparation Cranmer was chiefly responsible, appeared in 1553 at the end of the short reign of Edward VI. It contained forty-two articles of religion. The second, which came to be known as *The Thirty-Nine Articles,* was issued in 1563 and then again in 1571. This set represented a minimal revision of the first. In the revision Archbishop Parker made use of the *Württemberg Confession* (1552), a predominantly Lutheran document (but with minor Calvinist emphases) prepared for submission to the Council of Trent.[3]

Article XI of the *Forty-Two Articles* (1553) reads:

> Justification by only faith in Jesus Christ in that sense, as it is declared in the homily of justification, is a most certain and wholesome doctrine for Christian men.

The Latin has the famous phrase *sola fide—justificatio ex sola fide Jesu Christi.* Obviously this is too brief to be really helpful, and for this reason reference to the homily is necessary. What *faith alone* means is, however, partly brought out in Article XII which reads:

> Works done before the grace of Christ and the inspiration of his Spirit are not pleasant to God, forasmuch as they spring not of faith in Jesus Christ, neither do they make men meet to receive grace, or (as the School authorities say) deserve grace of congruity; but because they are not done as God hath willed and commanded them to be done, we doubt not, but they have the nature of sin.

This has more of a controversial flavor than Article XI, and it is aimed at a particular medieval understanding of merit.[4] This Article was retained in 1563, not as XII but as XIII.

Article XI of the *Thirty-Nine Articles* (1563) reads:

> We are accounted righteous before God, only for the merit of our Lord and Saviour Jesus Christ by faith, and not for our own works or deservings: wherefore, that we are justified by faith only is a most wholesome doctrine, and very full of comfort, as most largely is expressed in the Homily of Justification.

It appears that the original article was extended to making use of Article IV, *Württemberg Confession* (1552). Then a new article is added (XII):

> Albeit that good works which are the fruits of faith, and follow after justification, cannot put away our sins, and endure the severity of God's judgment; yet are they pleasing and acceptable to God in Christ, and do spring out necessarily of a true and lively faith: insomuch that by them a lively faith may be as evidently known as a tree discerned by the fruit.

This teaching is aimed at emphasizing good works as proceeding from true faith, but without claiming that they are good in themselves (as the Council of Trent had affirmed in Canon 32). Only in Christ are they acceptable to God.

Obviously the *Articles* of 1553 and 1563 agree in their emphasis on justification by faith. However, it will be observed that while those of 1553 contain no doctrine of forensic justification, those of 1563 do contain such a doctrine. The Latin text reads: *propter meritum Domini* (on account of the merit of Christ), referring to the decision of the judge in the heavenly court. This development is therefore much the same as that which occurred within Lutheranism from the *Augsburg Confession* (the influence of which is seen in the *Forty-Two Articles*) through the *Apology* to the *Formula of Concord.* And, in that English theologians were much influenced by Lutheran divines, it is to be expected.

Thus the question arises: Does the homily on justification (called the "Homily of Salvation" in the published *Homilies*) actually teach a doctrine of forensic imputation?[5] The answer will emerge as we examine the contents of the homily.

The primary purpose of the homily appears to be that of emphasizing and explaining that justification is by grace alone and by faith alone. Grace is the unmerited mercy of God revealed and offered to sinners in and through Jesus Christ; faith, the true faith that grasps Christ, is itself the gift of God worked in us by the Spirit. Thus justification is wholly the gift of God.

> Because all men be sinners and offenders against God, and breakers of his law and commandments, therefore can no man by his own acts, works, and deeds, seem they never so good, be justified and made righteous before God; but every man of necessity is constrained to seek for another righteousness or justification, to be received at God's own hands, that is to say, the remission, pardon, and forgiveness of his sins and trespasses in such things as he hath offended. And this justification or righteousness, which we so receive by God's mercy and Christ's merits, em-

braced by faith, is taken, accepted, and allowed of God for our perfect and full justification.

As Cranmer also explained:

It pleased our heavenly Father, of his infinite mercy, without any our desert or deserving, to prepare for us the most precious jewels of Christ's body and blood, whereby our ransom might be fully paid, the law fulfilled, and his justice fully satisfied. So that Christ is now the righteousness of all them that truly do believe in him. He for them paid their ransom by his death. He for them fulfilled the law in his life. So that now in him and by him every true Christian man may be called a fulfiller of the law; forasmuch as that which their infirmity lacketh Christ's justice hath supplied.

It is probable that Cranmer's reference to Christ fulfilling the law for those who believe is based on Melanchthon's teaching.[6]

Having made a special study of the early Fathers, both Greek and Latin, Cranmer went on to claim that such authors as Hilary, Ambrose, Basil and Augustine actually taught that salvation is wholly the gift of God and that our good works cannot save us.[7] However, along with many others of his time, Cranmer held that the teaching of the Fathers had been corrupted in the medieval period so that a doctrine of salvation by works had emerged with the Church. So he protested:

Justification is not the office of man, but of God. For man cannot make himself righteous by his own works, neither in part, nor in the whole; for that were the greatest arrogancy and presumption of man that Antichrist could set up against God, to affirm that a man might by his own works take away and purge his own sins, and so justify himself. But justification is the office of God only; and is not a thing which we render unto him, but which we receive of him; not which we give to him, but which we take of him, by his free mercy, and by the only merits of his most dearly beloved Son, our only Redeemer, Saviour, and Justifier, Jesus Christ. So that the true understanding of this doctrine, We be justified freely by faith without works, or that we be justified by faith in Christ only, is not that this our own act, to believe in Christ, or this our faith in Christ, which is within us, doth justify us and deserve our justification unto us; for that were to count ourselves to be justified by some act or virtue that is within ourselves. But the true understanding and meaning thereof is, that, although we hear God's word and believe it, although we have faith, hope, charity, repentance, dread, and fear of God within us, and do never so many good works thereunto, yet we must renounce the merit of all our said virtues of faith, hope, charity, and all our other virtues and good deeds, which we either have done, shall do, or can do, as things that be far too weak and insufficient and unperfect to deserve remission of our sins and our justification; and therefore we must trust only in God's mercy, and in that sacrifice which our High Priest and Saviour Christ Jesus, the Son of God, once offered for us upon the cross. . . .

Here again, as in the *Articles,* we see the protest against merit and on behalf of the free grace of God.

Like Luther, Cranmer believed that good works were necessary and that they proceed from the true believer quite naturally, since they are the fruit of the indwelling Spirit. The results of the grace of God should "move us to render ourselves unto God wholly with all our will, hearts, might and power; to serve him in all good deeds, obeying his commandments during our lives; to seek in all things his glory and honor, not our sensual pleasures and vain-glory."

While there is a strong insistence on the imputation of the righteousness of Christ (in the manner that Luther and the early Melanchthon emphasized), the idea of this righteousness as forensic is absent. The image of the heavenly courtroom is not used. Justification thus means, first, forgiveness and acceptance; then, second, it means inner renewal with outer manifestations of renewal. It would appear that for Cranmer justification is both acceptance with God through Christ and the actual process of being made righteous. "Truth it is that our own works do not justify us, to speak properly of our justification; that is to say, our works do not merit or deserve remission of our sins, and *make* us, of unjust, just before God; but God of his mere mercy, through the only merits and deservings of his son Jesus Christ, doth justify us."

Cranmer's doctrine is, therefore, to be distinguished from that of the Council of Trent in two areas. First, he claims that the righteousness of justification is imputed, not infused. And, second, he will have no doctrine of merit, not even for the good works of believers. Positively his position owes much to Luther and Melanchthon. It is well to remember that Article XI of 1563 was drafted by Archbishop Parker, and its reference to forensic righteousness need not be traced to Cranmer.

Richard Hooker (1554-1600)[8]

After the brief interlude of Mary Tudor's Roman Catholic reign (1553-1558), and until the English Civil War of the 1640s, it is fair to claim that English expositions of justification continued to affirm, against the teaching of the Council of Trent and its defenders, that the righteousness of justification is imputed not infused, extrinsic not intrinsic. It is the righteousness of the only mediator, Jesus Christ, the Just One. In fact, it is right to assert that the difference between the Anglican doctrine and Roman doctrine during the reigns of Elizabeth I, James I and Charles I was perceived to be by both sides the formal cause of justification,[9] "formal" meaning that which makes a thing to be what it is, as heat makes a thing hot. Thus, is it imputed or imparted righteousness?

To illustrate what is often called the classic Anglican position, we can do no better than notice the views of Richard Hooker, author of the famous treatise *Laws of Ecclesiastical Polity* and defender of classical Anglicanism against both Puritanism and Roman Catholicism. In his collected *Works* is a sermon, "A Learned Discourse of Justification," preached originally in 1586.[10] From this we can ascertain his doctrine of justification and sanctification.

Beginning with the assumption that all, including the Virgin Mary, are sinners and thus need a righteousness provided by God, he went on to declare how Christ is made the righteousness of men.

> There is a glorifying righteousness of men in the world to come: and there is a justifying and a sanctifying righteousness here. The righteousness, wherewith we shall be clothed in the world to come, is both perfect and inherent. That whereby here we are justified is perfect, but not inherent. That whereby we are sanctified, inherent, but not perfect.

Having declared his position in brief, he had to show where the differences between Roman Catholicism and Anglicanism were to be located.

Obviously there was some agreement between the Tridentine and Anglican positions. In the technical language of the day, they agreed that the grace of God in Jesus Christ is the meritorious cause of justification. God is the sole efficient cause of justification. Yet, in Hooker's words, "we disagree about the nature of the very essence of the medicine whereby Christ cureth our disease; about the manner of applying it; about the number and power of means, which God requireth of us for the effectual applying thereof to our soul's comfort." Here he is referring to the medicine of infused, inherent righteousness, to its application primarily through sacraments (baptism and especially the sacrament of penance), and its association with doctrines of mortal and venial sin, of merit and of purgatory. To him, it was "this maze the Church of Rome doth cause her followers to tread." It was his conviction that Rome had complicated and changed the relatively straightforward doctrine taught by St. Paul and St. James.

Hooker clearly distinguished between the righteousness of justification and the righteousness of sanctification.

> There are two kinds of Christian righteousness: the one without us, which we have by imputation; the other in us, which consisteth of faith, hope, charity, and other Christian virtues; and St. James doth prove that Abraham had not only the one, because the thing he believed was imputed unto him for righteousness; but also the other, because he offered up his son. God giveth us

both the one justice and the other: the one by accepting us for righteous in Christ; the other by working Christian righteousness in us. The proper and most immediate efficient cause in us of this latter, is, the spirit of adoption which we have received into our hearts.

Thus the formal cause of justification (forgiveness of sins and acceptance by God) is the imputed righteousness of Christ, while the formal cause of sanctification (inner renewal of the heart leading to Christian living) is the gift of the indwelling Holy Spirit.

Having distinguished the root from what grows or develops from it (in terms of sanctifying righteousness) he went on carefully to distinguish two kinds of sanctifying righteousness, "habitual and actual."

Habitual, that holiness wherewith our souls are inwardly endued, the same instant when first we begin to be the temples of the Holy Ghost; Actual, that holiness which afterward beautifieth all the parts and actions of our life, the holiness for which Enoch, Job, Zachary, Elizabeth, and other saints, are in Scriptures so highly commended.

Here is the use of Aristotelian terminology to bring clarification to the nature of sanctifying righteousness.

But how are justifying and sanctifying righteousness related? Which is first given and received? He answered:

that the Spirit, the virtues of the Spirit, the habitual justice, which is ingrafted, the external justice of Christ Jesus which is imputed, these we receive all at one and the same time; whensoever we have any of these, we have all; they go together. Yet since no man is justified except he believe, and no man believeth except he have faith, and no man hath faith, unless he have received the Spirit of Adoption forasmuch as these do necessarily infer justification, but justification doth of necessity presuppose them; we must needs hold that imputed righteousness, in dignity being the chiefest, is notwithstanding in order the last of all these, but actual righteousness, which is the righteousness of good works, succeedeth all, followeth after all, both in order and in time. Which thing being attentively marked, sheweth plainly how the faith of true believers cannot be divorced from hope and love; how faith is a part of sanctification, and yet unto justification necessary; how faith is perfected by good works, and yet no work of ours good without faith.

Here, it may be observed, there is a judicious marriage of the relationship with God in Christ and the relationship with the Church and world in love, both proceeding from grace. He met the challenge of

Tridentine Catholicism by claiming that for the Anglican, justifying righteousness and sanctifying righteousness belong together. Further, he clearly taught the importance of the sacraments in relation to both—baptism as the sacrament of justifying righteousness and the Lord's Supper as the sacrament of sanctifying righteousness.

Hooker did not specifically state that the imputed righteousness is to be understood forensically. However, other Anglican divines of this period did teach forensic imputation. Further, while Hooker chose to speak of justifying and sanctifying righteousness, other Anglicans followed the more typically Protestant way of speaking of only justification and sanctification. Both these tendencies are to be found in the sections "Of Justification and Faith" and "Of Sanctification and Good Works" in the *Articles of Religion agreed upon by the Archbishops and Bishops and the rest of the clergy of Ireland* (1615).[11]

Before describing the new doctrine of justification which emerged in the Church of England in the mid-seventeenth century, it is important to point out that the Anglican classical teaching on justification was held throughout the centuries by a significant number of Anglican clergy and people. It was held quite strongly by those evangelicals of the nineteenth century who opposed the Tractarian and Anglo-Catholic movement.[12] They certainly spoke of forensic imputation of Christ's righteousness and clearly distinguished justification from sanctification. However, though they sometimes referred to the "judicious Mr. Hooker," more often they referred to Puritan and Nonconformist expositions.

Evangelical teaching was given very clear expression in the writings of Bishop J. C. Ryle, a master of concise prose.[13] Here is how he defined justification and sanctification in his book *Holiness* (1877), which has often been reprinted.

(a) Justification is the *reckoning* and counting a man to be righteous for the sake of another, even Jesus Christ the Lord. Sanctification is the actual *making* a man inwardly righteous, though it may be in a very feeble degree.

(b) The righteousness we have by our justification is *not our own,* but the everlasting perfect righteousness of our great mediator Christ, imputed to us, and made our own by faith. The righteousness we have by sanctification is *our own* righteousness, imparted, inherent, and wrought in us by the Holy Spirit, but mingled with much infirmity and imperfection.

(c) In justification our own works have no place at all, and simple faith in Christ is the one thing needful. In sanctification our own works are of vast importance, and God bids us fight, and watch, and pray, and strive, and take pains, and labor.

(d) Justification is a finished and complete work, and a man is perfectly justified the moment he believes. Sanctification is an imperfect work, comparatively, and will never be perfected until we reach Heaven.

(e) Justification admits of no growth or increase: a man is as much justified the hour he first comes to Christ by faith as he will be to all eternity. Sanctification is eminently a progressive work, and admits of continual growth and enlargement so long as a man lives.

(f) Justification has special reference to our *persons*, our standing in God's sight, and our deliverance from guilt. Sanctification has special reference to our *natures*, and the moral renewal of our hearts.

(g) Justification gives us our title to Heaven, and boldness to enter in. Sanctification gives us our meetness for Heaven, and prepares us to enjoy it when we dwell there.

(h) Justification is the act of God *about* us, and is not easily discerned by others. Sanctification is the work of God *within* us, and cannot be hid in its outward manifestation from the eyes of men.

It is probably accurate to claim that the majority of evangelical Anglicans have continued to view the matter in this or a similar manner. Where Ryle and twentieth-century evangelical Anglicans differ from Hooker (and from other classical Anglicans such as Lancelot Andrewes) is that the latter clearly expound the doctrine in an ecclesiological and sacramental context, whereas the former tend to see it in individualistic terms.

A New Anglican Doctrine of Justification

Thomas Barlow, bishop of Lincoln from 1675 to 1691, who taught the classical Anglican doctrine of justification, noted that an alternative and, to his mind, erroneous teaching emerged around 1640 and gained momentum through the civil war and in the Protectorate before the restoration of the monarchy in 1660. To a curate in his diocese he wrote:[14]

> Before the late unhappy Rebellion (at least all I have yet met with) such as Bishop Jewel, Hooker, Reynolds, Whittaker, Davenant, Field, Downham, John White, etc., do constantly prove, and vindicate the imputation of our blessed Saviour's righteousness. . . . So that, in truth, it is only you, and some Neotericks, who (since the year 1640) deny such imputation . . . to the prejudice of Truth, and the scandal of our Church and Religion.

Barlow well understood that behind the new doctrine lay a genuine concern to unite that which is believed with that which is done and lived and to bring together faith and genuine works of love.

Justification by faith alone (as expounded in the emotive context of a nation divided in its loyalties and then actually engaged in civil war) appeared to some devout Anglicans and at least several Puritans (notably Richard Baxter)[15] to have become merely a verbal formula unproductive of holy and disciplined living. The careless exposition of some soldiers in the army of Parliament together with the teaching of some of the separatists and sects seemed to confirm the fear that both doctrinal and practical antinomianism were gaining ground.

The new doctrine of justification, as taught by such men as Jeremy Taylor (1613-1667), Henry Hammond (1605-1660) and Herbert Thorndike (1598-1672), must be seen in this context of national disorder and the desire to relate faith to "holy living" (a phrase used by Taylor in two famous books).[16] At the center of this doctrine is the denial that the formal cause of justification is the imputed righteousness of Christ and the insistence that where there is true justification from God there is also genuine repentance and pursuit of holy living in the one justified.

The work of Jesus Christ as Savior of the world and specifically his mediatorial righteousness was seen as that without which there could not be any acceptance or justification of sinners. The active and passive righteousness of the exalted Christ (arising from his perfect life and sacrificial, atoning death) was said to be the meritorious cause (not the formal cause) of justification. The perfect righteousness of the One who sits at the Father's right hand is not imputed to the believer; rather, it is because of this that justification can occur. What God actually counts or reckons to the sinner as a righteousness acceptable to himself is the faith of the Christian. This belief was based on Genesis 15:6 where it is said of Abraham, "He believed in the LORD; and he (God) counted it to him for righteousness." (Cf. Paul's use of this text in Romans 4 and Galatians 3, together with James 2:23.)

Faith was seen not as the faith which merely believes (for devils have such faith), but as a trust in God associated with repentance and turning away from sin. True faith expressed itself in faithfulness to God and the way of Christ. Seeing the beginnings of such genuine faith (which they insisted was the gift of God in that it was promoted by the work of the Holy Spirit within the soul of man), God reckoned or accounted such a sinner to be righteous in his sight; thus his sins were forgiven, and he was adopted into the family of God. In this view there is no justification unless there is the beginning of true faith which expresses itself in new attitudes and works. Thus justification was presented as both an event—God's acceptance and forgiveness of the sinner—and as a process of realizing righteousness in holy living. The possibility always remained that faithfulness to God would disappear and thus justification could be temporarily or finally lost. (This aspect of their teaching led to the charge of Arminianism.)

To those who held the classical Anglican position (e.g., Thomas Barlow) or the classic high Calvinist position (e.g., John Owen), this novel way of stating the doctrine of justification seemed to confuse the issues at stake between Roman Catholicism and Protestantism, as well as appearing to make justification dependent not ultimately on grace but on human initiative. Further, it was argued that God was portrayed as accepting something imperfect—human faith—as the basis for justification. How could a holy and righteous God do this? Those who taught the new doctrine defended it on the ground that it harmonized the teaching of St. Paul and St. James and that it was productive of holy living. They fully recognized that the human faith which was imputed by God for righteousness was not perfect faith, but they stressed that it was acceptable because of the meritorious faith and righteousness of Christ. Further, they pointed out that the faith by which Abraham was justified was not perfect faith!

Thus from the seventeenth century onwards there were within the Church of England (and later within Anglicanism) two differing doctrines of justification—both claiming to be faithful to the Scriptures and in accord with the formularies of the Church. Even as evangelical Anglicans of the nineteenth century claimed to be teaching the classical Anglican position, the Tractarians and Anglo-Catholics of the same period claimed to be teaching that doctrine which was expounded by the later Caroline divines such as Jeremy Taylor and Herbert Thorndike. It was the Anglo-Catholics who were responsible for the printing of the works of these seventeenth-century divines in the Library of Anglo-Catholic Theology, even as it was the evangelicals who initiated the reprinting of the works of the sixteenth-century Protestant writers in the volumes of the Parker Society.[17]

Appendix
The Irish Anglican Articles of 1615

Of Iustification and Faith.

34. We are accounted righteous before God, onely for the merit of our Lord and Saviour Iesus Christ, applied by faith; and not for our owne workes or merits. And this righteousnes, which we so receiue of Gods mercie and Christs merits, imbraced by faith, is taken, accepted, and allowed of God, for our perfect and full iustification.

35. Although this iustification be free vnto vs, yet it commeth not so freely vnto vs, that there is no ransome paid therefore at all. God shewed his great mercie in deliuering vs from our former captiuitie, without requiring of any ransome to be payd, or amends to be made on our parts; which thing by vs had been vnpossible to be done. And whereas all the world was not able of themselues to pay any part towards their ransome, it pleased our heavenly Father of his infinite mercie without any desert of ours, to prouide for vs the most precious merits of his owne Sonne, whereby our ransome might be fully payd, the lawe fulfilled, and

his iustice fully satisfied. So that Christ is now the righteousnes of all them that truely beleeue in him. Hee for them payd their ransome by his death. He for them fulfilled the lawe in his life; that now in him, and by him euerie true Christian man may be called a fulfiller of the lawe : forasmuch as that which our infirmitie was not able to effect, Christs iustice hath performed. And thus the iustice and mercie of God doe embrace each other: the grace of God not shutting out the iustice of God in the matter of our iustification; but onely shutting out the iustice of man (that is to say, the iustice of our own workes) from being any cause of deseruing our iustification.

36. When we say that we are iustified by Faith onely, we doe not meane that the said iustifying faith is alone in man, without true Repentance, Hope, Charity, and the feare of God (for such a faith is dead, and cannot iustifie), either do we meane, that this our act to beleeue in Christ, or this our faith in Christ, which is within vs, doth of it selfe iustifie vs, or deserue our iustification vnto vs, (for that were to account our selues to bee iustified by the vertue or dignitie of some thing that is within our selues :) but the true vnderstanding and meaning thereof is that although we heare Gods word and beleeue it, although we haue Faith, Hope, Charitie, Repentance, and the feare of God within us, and adde neuer so many good workes thereunto: yet wee must renounce the merit of all our said vertues, of Faith, Hope, Charitie, and all our other vertues, and good deeds which we either haue done, shall doe, or can doe, as things that be farre too weake and vnperfect, and vnsufficient to deserue remission of our sinnes, and our iustification: and therefore we must trust onely in Gods mercie, and the merits of his most dearely beloued Sonne, our onely Redeemer, Sauiour, and Iustifier Iesus Christ. Neuerthelesse, because Faith doth directly send vs to Christ for our iustification, and that by faith giuen vs of God wee embrace the promise of Gods mercie, and the remission of our sinnes, (which thing none other of our vertues or workes properly doth:) therefore the Scripture vseth to say, that *Faith without workes;* and the auncient fathers of the Church to the same purpose, that *onely Faith* doth iustifie vs.

37. By iustifying Fatih wee vnderstand not onely the common beleefe of the Articles of Christian Religion, and the perswasion of the truth of Gods worde in generall: but also a particular application of the gratious promises of the Gospell, to the comfort of our owne soules: whereby we lay hold on Christ, with all his benefits, hauing an earnest trust and confidence in God, that he will be merciful vnto vs for his onely Sonnes sake. So that a true beleeuer may bee certaine, by the assurance of faith, of the forgiuenesse of his sinnes, and of his euerlasting saluation by Christ.

38. A true liuely iustifying faith, and the sanctifying spirit of God, is not extinguished, nor vanisheth away in the regenerate, either finally or totally.

Of Sanctification and Good Workes.

39. All that are iustified, are likewise sanctified: their faith being alwaies accompanied with true Repentance and good Workes.

40. Repentance is a gift of God, whereby a godly sorrow is wrought in the heart of the faithfull, for offending God their mercifull Father by their former transgressions, together with a constant resolution for the time to come to cleaue unto God, and to lead a new life.

41. Albeit that good workes, which are the fruits of faith, and follow after iustification, cannot make satisfaction for our sinnes, and endure the seueritie of Gods iudgement: yet are they pleasing to God and accepted of him in Christ, and doe spring from a true and liuely faith, which by them is to be discerned, as a tree by the fruite.

42. The workes which God would haue his people to walke in, are such as he hath commaunded in his holy Scripture, and not such workes as men haue deuised out of their own braine, of a blind zeale, and deuotion, without the warrant of the worde of God.

43. The regenerate cannot fulfil the lawe of God perfectly in this life. For in many things we offend all: and if we say, we haue no sinne, wee deceaue our selues, and the truth is not in vs.

44. Not euerie heynous sinne willingly committed after baptisme, is sinne against the holy Ghost, and vnpardonable. And therefore to such as fall into sinne after baptisme, place for repentance is not to be denied.

45. Voluntary workes, besides ouer and aboue God's commandements, which they call workes of Supererogation, cannot be taught without arrogancie and impietie. For by them men doe declare that they doe not onely render vnto God as much as they are bound to doe, but that they doe more for his sake then of bounden duty is required.

10   The Wesleyan View

Martin Luther and John Wesley invite comparison. Both were intensely zealous in religious duty before they discovered that justification is by faith and not by religious achievement. Each one experienced a great change in his life and ministry after his submission in faith to the Father of our Lord Jesus Christ. Further, both Luther and Wesley had, and still have, a tremendous influence over thousands of people. And each, in somewhat different ways, made justification by faith central to their understanding of Christian doctrine. But there were differences. Luther saw the corruption of human nature by sin to be more radical than did Wesley. And conversely while Wesley believed that full sanctification was possible on earth, Luther believed that it was only attainable in the age to come.

     John Wesley (1703-1791) became a great evangelist, a brilliant organizer and a popular theologian.[1] He was born into the family of a pious Church of England clergyman, and he died an ordained priest of the same Church. But before his death he set in motion a movement which is now represented by the worldwide family of churches called Methodist. Since these churches adopted as their theological basis certain of his writings, we shall concentrate in this chapter on the exposition of his teaching. This has particular features which distinguish it from the various types of doctrine we have already encountered. Further, in adapted or popular form, this teaching has been tremendously influential for thousands of "Arminian" Christians.

Faith and Good Works

Following an intensely religious upbringing in the parsonage, Wesley went to Oxford University where eventually he was elected as a Fellow of Lincoln College. His pilgrimage as a Christian was deeply influenced by the famous book *Holy Living and Holy Dying* by Jeremy

Taylor, the Caroline divine. The high ideal of duty presented by Taylor fired the mind of young Wesley, who resolved to dedicate himself wholly to God and seek to fulfill the law of Christ. His dedication and self-denial was intensified when he later read *The Imitation of Christ* by Thomas á Kempis; from this he learned that God wants purity of heart as well as external obedience. Further challenge came from William Law through his *Christian Perfection* and *A Serious Call to a Devout and Holy Life*. From these books Wesley gained the conviction that it was possible by grace to achieve perfection as a Christian; this belief he held all his life.

There was no stopping his zeal to perform deeds of mercy and to impose discipline of body for the good of the soul. After involvement with the poor and needy of Oxford he set sail for Georgia, longing for a greater opportunity to do good and thereby help to save his soul. Insofar as he had a doctrine of justification at this stage it was of the same kind as that taught by Jeremy Taylor and the prominent Anglican divines in the period after 1662 (see Chapter 9). It involved the conviction that God will not declare righteous those who are not doing all within their power to be righteous. Not faith alone, for that leads to antinomianism, but faith and works lead to holiness, he believed. But he was a failure as a missionary in Georgia. He had no good news and so had no success among either the white settlers or the native red Indians.

Wesley's own spiritual pilgrimage was so intense and so concerned, ultimately, with himself that he could not bring hope or faith to others. It has been claimed that from 1720 to 1738 "self-love was at the very center of his life. His neighbor and his neighbor's needs, though they engaged by far the greater portion of his activity, had no significance in and of themselves, but were important only insofar as they contributed to his own salvation."[2] On February 1, 1738 he looked back on his unhappy time in Georgia and wrote in his journal:

> Behold I gave all my goods to feed the poor. . . . I have labored more abundantly than they all . . . I have thrown up my friends, reputation, ease, country; I have put my life in my hand, wandering into strange lands; I have given my body to be devoured by the deep, parched up with heat, consumed with toil and weariness, or whatsoever God should please to bring upon me. But does all this . . . make me acceptable to God? Does all I ever did or can know, say, give, do, or suffer, justify me in his sight?[3]

The answer to the last question was No, as he was soon fully to recognize.

Salvation by Faith

A sense of failure in Georgia, together with a deep impression made upon him by the Moravians, led to a great change in Wesley's view of

Christianity. The Moravians, Pietists who had their origin in Europe, sought to recall Lutheranism from mere doctrinal orthodoxy to a living faith in Jesus and a devotion to him.[4] From the Moravians, Wesley gained insight into the need to trust in Jesus and in Jesus alone for salvation. One of their number, Peter Böhler, told him: "Preach faith till you have it; and then, because you have it, you will preach faith."[5]

For May 24, 1738 he recorded in his journal:

> In the evening I went very unwillingly to a society in Aldersgate Street, where one was reading Luther's preface to the Epistle to the Romans. About a quarter before nine, while he was describing the change which God works in the heart through faith in Christ, I felt my heart strangely warmed. I felt that I did trust in Christ, Christ alone for salvation, and an assurance was given me that he had taken away my sins, even mine, and saved me from the law of sin and death.[6]

To call this a conversion to God is perhaps to misunderstand. But certainly Wesley received a definite assurance of personal salvation on this occasion, and he recognized very clearly that faith, genuine faith, is the key to salvation and regeneration.

The change in his thinking and approach to the quest for salvation is seen in the sermon he preached at Oxford on June 18, of the same year. Let us note how he defined faith:

> It acknowledges Christ's death as the only sufficient means of redeeming man from eternal death, and his resurrection as the restoration of us all to life and immortality; inasmuch as he "was delivered for our sins and rose again for our justification." Christian faith is then, not only an assent to the whole gospel of Christ, but also a full reliance on the blood of Christ: a trust in the merits of his life, death, and resurrection; a recumbency upon him as our atonement and our life, as *given for us,* and *living in us;* and, in consequence hereof, a closing with him, and cleaving to him, as our "wisdom, sanctification, and redemption," or, in one word, our salvation.[7]

And how, we ask, did he define salvation? It is,

> a salvation from sin, and the consequences of sin, both often expressed in the word *justification;* which, taken in the largest sense, implies a deliverance from guilt and punishment, by the atonement of Christ actually applied onto the soul of the sinner now believing on him, and a deliverance from the power of sin, through Christ *formed in his heart.* So that he who is thus justified, or saved by faith, is indeed *born again.* He is *born again of the*

Spirit unto a new life . . . until at length he comes unto "a perfect man, unto the measure of the stature of the fullness of Christ."[8]

By adopting the Pietist approach to salvation by faith, Wesley certainly turned away from the common contemporary Anglican way of describing justification in terms of faith and works. He also turned towards the Reformed or Calvinist position, describing his own position as "within a hair's breadth of Calvinism."[9] This description is not, as we shall see, entirely accurate.

Justification by Faith

One of the standard sermons of Methodism is one entitled "Justification by Faith," written by Wesley.[10] Its contents represent a succinct summary of the Wesleyan doctrine.

1. The ground of justification. Wesley never wrote a book on the atonement, but he held that the death and resurrection of Jesus Christ were the ground or basis for the justification of sinners. He saw the first human beings as related to God in a covenant of works. Adam, the father of the race, and Eve, his wife, were to obey God's perfect law of love, and God was to give to them eternal life. Adam chose to disobey the Lord, and sin entered into the world. "His soul died, was separated from God; separate from whom the soul has no more life than the body has when separate from the soul. His body likewise became corruptible and mortal, so that death took hold on this also. And being already dead in spirit, dead to God, dead in sin, he hastened on to death everlasting; to the destruction both of body and soul, in the fire never to be quenched." Everything seemed lost, but the eternal Son of God became man and "another common Head of mankind, a second general Parent and Representative of the whole human race." He suffered in our place and made atonement for our sins. "By the sacrifice for sin made by the second Adam, as the Representative of us all, God is so far reconciled to all the world, that he hath given them a new covenant; the plain condition whereof being once fulfilled, 'there is no more condemnation' for us, but 'we are justified freely by his grace, through the redemption that is in Jesus Christ.' " Unlike Luther and Calvin, Wesley was explicitly and dogmatically clear that Jesus Christ had died to make atonement for each and every human being in all times and places.

2. The nature of justification. Justification does not mean to be made just and righteous, Wesley insisted. Such a process is sanctification. "The plain scriptural notion of justification is pardon, the forgiveness of sins. It is the act of God the Father, whereby, for the sake of the propitiation made by the blood of his Son, he 'sheweth forth his righteousness' (or mercy) 'by the remission of the sins that are past.' " God does not impute or reckon sin to the condemnation of the believer. "His sins, all his past sins, in thought, word, and deed, are covered, are blotted out, shall not be remembered or mentioned against him, any more than if they had not been." He is accepted in Christ and God looks upon him "as if he had never sinned."

We note here that Wesley did not include the idea of the imputation of the perfect righteousness of Christ to the believer as part of the Father's declaration of justification. Justification is only forgiveness and acceptance. Probably the reason why he rejected this Lutheran and Calvinist emphasis was that he believed that it savoured of doctrinal antinomianism. In the 1690s there had been a bitter controversy over the doctrine of grace, and by some this doctrine of imputed righteousness was seen as a way of escaping from the demands of the life of holiness.[11] "Such a notion of justification," wrote Wesley, "is neither reconcilable to reason nor Scripture."

3. The identity of those who are justified. Who are actually justified? The answer is simple: "ungodly of every kind and degree and none but the ungodly." It is not the case (as Wesley earlier had held) that "a man must be sanctified, that is, holy, before he can be justified." But what about the many "good" people who do so many helpful and kind deeds? These good works, said Wesley, may well be good and profitable to men, but it does not follow that they are profitable, strictly speaking, in the sight of God. To make his meaning clear he set out this syllogism:

> No works are good, which are not done as God hath willed and commanded them to be done:
> But no works done before justification are done as God hath willed and commanded them to be done:
> Therefore, no works done before justification are good.

Here, at least, it may be claimed that his teaching is in harmony with that of Luther.

4. How are the ungodly justified? There is but one simple answer: faith. "Justifying faith implies, not only a divine evidence or conviction that 'God was in Christ reconciling the world unto himself' but a sure trust and confidence that Christ died for *my* sins, that he loved *me,* and gave himself for *me.*" But why does God say, faith alone? The short answer is, to eliminate pride. "He that cometh unto God by this faith, must fix his eye singly on his own wickedness, on his guilt and helplessness, without having the least regard to any supposed good in himself, to any virtue or righteousness whatsoever. He must come as a *mere sinner,* inwardly and outwardly, self-destroyed and self-condemned, bringing nothing to God but ungodliness only, pleading nothing of his own but sin and misery."

Though Wesley was deeply conscious that saving faith is a gift of God, he held that it is available to all who hear the gospel. While God acts in prevenient grace to offer salvation and to make the hearer able to respond, the decision to respond is that of the hearer. The human will is not forced into faith; at most, it is persuaded into faith by the constraining love of God.

It is because of Wesley's insistence on the universality of Christ's atonement and on the free decision of sinful man to believe in Christ that Wesleyan theology has often been classed as Arminian. Of course it is not identical, but there are sufficient similarities for the teaching of Wesley to be coupled with that of Jacob Arminius.

The New Birth

Wesley rightly held that it was most important to distinguish justification from regeneration.

> Though it be allowed that justification and the new birth are, in point of time, inseparable from each other, yet they are easily distinguished, as being not the same, but things of a widely different nature. Justification implies only a relative, the new birth a real, change. God in justifying us does something *for* us; in begetting us again, he does the work *in* us. The former changes our outward relation to God so that of enemies we become children; by the latter our inmost souls are changed, so that of sinners we become saints.[12]

From the time when he had read Jeremy Taylor's *Holy Living and Holy Dying* at Oxford, Wesley had recognized that God calls the Christian to wholehearted commitment to a search for perfection in the love of God and human beings. His discovery of the evangelical understanding of the new birth served, not to cancel his settled belief, but to give it new life and potency. He saw the new birth as the placing and release within the heart of the believer of great spiritual power, bringing illumination, love, faith and hope. Few writers, it may be observed, in the English language have exceeded Wesley in his powerful descriptions of the tremendous internal changes caused by being born of God. For example, writing of the born-again person, he said:

> His ears are now opened, and the voice of God no longer calls in vain. He hears and obeys the heavenly calling; he knows the voice of his Shepherd. All his spiritual senses being now awakened, he has a clear intercourse with the invisible world; and hence he knows more and more of the things which before it could not "enter into his heart to conceive." He now knows what the peace of God is; what is joy in the Holy Ghost; what the love of God which is shed abroad in the hearts of them that believe in him through Jesus Christ. Thus the veil being removed which before intercepted the light and voice, the knowledge and love of God, he who is born of the Spirit dwelleth in love, "dwelleth in God, and God in him."[13]

Sermons which portray regeneration in such a way are plentiful among his collected works. He who reads these cannot but be very impressed by the intensity of Wesley's view of the tremendous spiritual reality of the divine work of regeneration.

Because he took the new birth so seriously he could not escape what seemed to him the clear implications of 1 John 3:9: "No one who is born of God will continue to sin, because God's seed remains in him; he cannot go on sinning, because he has been born of God." He would not concede that there were any qualifiers to be added to the pure words of God. This verse was to be taken at its face value. Sin meant "an actual, voluntary transgression of the law; of the revealed, written law of God; of any commandment of God, acknowledged to be such at the time that it is transgressed." And he maintained that,

> "Whosoever is born of God" while he abideth in faith and love, and in the spirit of prayer and thanksgiving, not only doth not, but cannot, thus commit sin. So long as he thus believeth in God through Christ, and loves him, and is pouring out his heart before him, he cannot voluntarily transgress any command of God, either by speaking or acting what he knows God hath forbidden, so long that seed which remaineth in him, that loving, praying thankful faith, compels him to refrain from whatsoever he knows to be an abomination in the sight of God.[14]

The key to "not committing sin" is not only being born of God, but also abiding in faith.

Wesley was well aware that people who are born of God do commit sin, and he offered an interesting analysis of how this actually occurs in the born-again believer.

(1) The divine seed of loving, conquering faith, remains in him that is born of God. "He keepeth himself," by the grace of God, and "cannot commit sin."

(2) A temptation arises; whether from the world, the flesh or the devil, it matters not.

(3) The Spirit of God gives him warning that sin is near, and bids him more abundantly watch unto prayer.

(4) He gives way, in some degree, to the temptation, which now begins to grow pleasing to him.

(5) The Holy Spirit is grieved; his faith is weakened; and his love of God grows cold.

(6) The Spirit reproves him more sharply and saith, "This is the way, walk thou in it."

(7) He turns away from the painful voice of God and listens to the pleasing voice of the tempter.

(8) Evil desire begins and spreads in his soul, till faith and love

vanish away; he is then capable of committing outward sin, the power of the Lord being departed from him.[15]

This quotation and the earlier discussion indicate that while the new birth does not free the believer from the possibility of falling completely from grace, it does, however, provide power over sin if he will make use of it and a new principle of goodness if he will implement it.

Perfection or Full Sanctification

Even as a baby boy is born of its mother in a brief time but takes many years to grow to manhood, so a sinner is born of God in a brief moment but takes a long time to grow up into that spiritual manhood or maturity to which God calls him in Christ. The state of perfect love, entire sanctification or Christian perfection is attainable on earth by the believer, taught Wesley. He was deeply conscious that "without holiness no man can see the Lord." He saw full sanctification as "the grand depositum which God has lodged with the people called Methodist; and for the sake of propagating this chiefly he appeared to have raised us up."[16]

Wesley wrote *The Plain Account of Christian Perfection*,[17] but the theme is found in many of his sermons, sometimes explicitly (e.g., as in "Christian Perfection") and sometimes implicitly (e.g., as those on the Sermon on the Mount). For Wesley, justification and regeneration signify a completed act of God. In place of the traditional Protestant idea of growth (from regeneration) *towards* holiness—that is, a process *prior to* its attainment—he substituted a growth *in* holiness, *subsequent to* its attainment (in regeneration). Thus Wesleyan ethics are ethics of realization rather than of aspiration. Having rejected the doctrine of the imputation of the active righteousness of Christ to the believer, he looked to the believer in the power of the Spirit to grow *in* righteousness, given at the new birth. He believed (both before and after his heart-warming experience) that final salvation includes moral attainment and personal purity as basic and essential elements. Thus obedience to the law of God in life is absolutely necessary, and perfect love is the fulfillment of the law. Full sanctification or Christian perfection is the end of growth in righteousness/holiness and constitutes the final condition for salvation and entrance into the presence of God through Christ. It is purity of motive, a life wholly governed by the love of God. In body and mind, however, the fully sanctified Christian is still finite and so is not infallible in knowledge and judgment; and he has no exemption from ignorance, bodily infirmity or temptation.

Full sanctification is by faith and occurs after some time in the process of growth *in* holiness. It is not always possible to pinpoint the moment, and it may well occur immediately before death. But the evidence of its occurrence is the existence of perfect love in the heart.[18] This state of perfection is not static but admits of growth in the intensity and scope of love. As the state of justification/regeneration can be lost through lack of faith, so can the state of full sanctification where it is reached before the point of death. No one is actually finally and fully saved until he enters into the presence of his Lord after death.

In the history of Methodism (and groups which have developed from it) the doctrines of Wesley have not always been presented in the way he (and his brother Charles) expressed them. In particular, the quest for "Christian perfection" has often been misunderstood and minimized through the presentation of "the second blessing" by which one enters into a state of perfect love and wholehearted commitment.[19]

Part 3: Contemporary

11 Newman and Schmaus

In this chapter we examine the teaching of two Roman Catholic theologians. One lived and died in the last century, but his real influence within his Church has been this century. The other has taught in Germany since the Second World War and represents a progressive conservative approach. Both have written books on the topic of justification—the former in a written edition of lectures he delivered, and the other as the last volume in a six-volume series on *Dogma*. The first is John Henry Newman, and the second is Michael Schmaus. It would have been interesting to include Hans Küng, but he no longer represents an official Roman Catholic position; and further, his book on justification is in fact a comparative study of the teaching of the Council of Trent and of Karl Barth.

John Henry Newman
Newman's impact has come particularly in the period before and after the Second Vatican Council. He entered the Church of Rome in 1845 after achieving prominence within the Church of England as a leader of the Tractarian movement. The Pope made him a cardinal in 1879, but his theological methods differed from the dominant, scholastic methods of the theologians of his new Church. He worked in the Anglican way, making much use of the Scriptures and the early Fathers; he used Aristotelian categories and looked to Thomas Aquinas as his guide. So the mood within the Church of Rome had to change for Newman truly to be heard.[1]

In 1837 Newman gave a course of lectures in the university church of St. Mary, Oxford, on the topic of justification. He did this partly as a response to a challenge made in the pages of the *Christian Observer*, the monthly magazine of the evangelicals. Was he a Protestant or papist? Did he believe in justification by works?[2] The lectures appeared in print as *Lectures on Justification* (1838). At this stage in his pilgrimage, Newman held that neither the dogma of Trent nor the classic Protestant statements on justification were wholly correct. Further, he had come to hold a very high view of regeneration through his study of the Greek Fathers, stressing the full presence of the living God in the soul of man. At baptism this great gift enters into the Christian, he said. He saw definite links between justification and regeneration. In fact, he complained that "it is the fashion of the day to sever these two from one another, which God has joined, the seal and the impression, justification and renewal" (p. 202). It was his conviction that the *Thirty-Nine Articles of Religion* and other formularies of the Church of England supported the position he adopted. He believed as he read both the letters of Paul and the treatises of St. Athanasius that justification was both a declaring and a making righteous of the believing sinner. The external and the internal work of God must be kept together.[3]

Justification as the glorious voice of the Lord declaring us to be righteous. Basing himself on clear Old Testament teaching, Newman argued that the word which proceeds from God's mouth does not return to him void, but accomplishes that which he pleases. God said, "Let there be light" and there was light. Jesus, the Word made flesh, called Lazarus from the grave and Lazarus rose from the dead. Therefore when God "utters the command 'Let the soul be just,' it becomes just." "Justification is 'the glorious Voice of the Lord' declaring us to be righteous." That it is primarily a declaration, not a making, is sufficiently clear, Newman argued, from this one argument—that it is the justification of a sinner, of one who has been a sinner, "and the past cannot be reversed except by *accounting* it reversed."

Yet, as has already been indicated, it is not only a declaration about the past; it is also a declaration about the present. Concerning the past, justification "supposes a judicial process, that is, an accuser, a judgment seat and a prisoner"; thus God "declares, acknowledges, and accepts us as holy." He recognizes us as his own and publicly repeals the sentence of wrath and penal statutes which lie against us."

The declaration about the present is related to the power of the Word of the Lord. What is declared is brought into reality. Righteousness is placed in the human heart, for "the Voice of the Lord is mighty in operation, the Voice of the Lord is a glorious Voice." The soul is actually made righteous. Precisely how this is accomplished by the Lord we shall examine later.

Here is Newman's own summary of this theme of the voice of the Lord:

It appears that justification is an announcement or fiat of Almighty God breaking upon the gloom of our natural state as the Creative Word upon chaos; that it *declares* the soul righteous, and in that declaration, on the one hand, conveys *pardon* for its past sins, and on the other *makes* it actually *righteous*. That it is a declaration, has been made evident from its including, as all allow, an amnesty for the past; for past sins are removable only by imputation of righteousness. And that it involves an actual creation in righteousness has been argued from the analogy of Almighty God's doings in Scripture, in which we find his words were represented as effective.[4]

So he who is justified becomes just, or he who is declared righteous is thereby actually made righteous. Newman claimed that this teaching was in harmony with the *Articles of Religion*, numbers 11 and 13.

In another lecture he said the following:

> The great benefit of justification, as all will allow, is this one thing—the transference of the soul from the kingdom of darkness into the kingdom of Christ. We may, if we will, divide this event into parts, and say that it is *both* pardon *and* renovation, but such a division is merely mental, and does not affect the transit (so to speak) itself, which is but one act. If a man is saved from drowning, you may, if you will, say he is *both* rescued from the water *and* brought into atmospheric air; this is a discrimination in words not in things. He cannot be brought out of the water, which he cannot breathe, *except* by entering the air which he can breathe. In like manner, there is in fact no middle state between a state of *wrath* and a state of *holiness*. In justifying, God takes away what is past, *by* bringing in what is new. He takes us out of the fire by lifting us in his everlasting hands, and enwrapping us in his own glory.[5]

What God has joined, says Newman, let not theologians divide asunder.

Justification as the presence of God in the soul. Newman asked the question: What is the difference, the real difference, between a justified man and a nonjustified man? He believed that the typical Protestant answer was an answer without real substance, for it referred only to thoughts in God's mind. As he put the matter:

> If the only real difference between a justified man and a man unjustified, be Almighty God's thoughts concerning him, then those who are justified are justified from eternity, for God sees the end from the beginning. They are in a justified state even from the hour of their birth.[6]

Justification must be something real on earth! To say that "our justification consists in union with Christ, or reconciliation with God, is an intelligible and fair answer," but it still does not tell us what is meant by this *union*. And this we surely need to know.

If we say that faith is that which unites the soul to Christ, that faith is the reality which is acceptable to God in the heart of the sinner, then the question arises: What is it about such faith that makes it acceptable to God? Why is it superior to unbelief? The answer must be the grace of God. By divine grace alone true faith exists and is acceptable to God. So if Protestants were to give a real answer they must speak in terms of union with Christ, internal faith and the grace of God in the soul. As matters stood, the traditional Protestant doctrine was "a system of words without ideas and of distinctions without arguments."

Newman believed that the traditional Roman Catholic answer was a real or meaningful answer, but nevertheless not a true answer. This answer claims that justification is inherent righteousness, spiritual renovation. It is the *result* of the grace of God in the soul, or the sanctifying effects of the regenerating power of the Holy Spirit. Newman shared some of the disgust of Protestants at the way the grace of God was described in (popular?) contemporary Roman Catholicism. He claimed that it "views or tends to view the influences of grace, not as the operations of a Living God, but as something to bargain about, and buy, and traffick with, as if religion were, not an approach to things above us, but a commerce with our equals concerning things we can master." No doubt he was thinking of the way the sacraments were described and received. Nevertheless, inner renewal and spiritual renovation make sense and thus point to a real answer.

Why was this answer incorrect? A brief reply is that it referred to the results and not to the essence of justification, which is a heavenly gift. Newman amassed biblical references (such as Romans 5:17, which refers to "the gift of righteousness") in order to show that righteousness is a gift received in our hearts. Then he summarized his thoughts in these words:

> That the righteousness, on which we are called righteous, or are justified, that in which justification results or consists, which conveys or applies the great gospel privileges, that this justifying principle, though within us, as it must be, if it is to separate us from the world, yet is not *of* us or *in* us, not any quality or act of our minds, not faith, not renovation, not obedience, not any thing cognizable by man, but a certain *divine* gift in which all these qualifications are included.[7]

Newman argued that it was possible to define this divine gift more precisely. "I mean," he wrote, "the habitation in us of God the Father and the Word Incarnate through the Holy Ghost." To be justified is "to receive the Divine Presence within us and be made a Temple of the Holy Ghost." So we see how, for Newman, his high doctrine of regeneration is united with his doctrine of justification. Regeneration, the indwelling of God in the human soul, is part of, the human side of, justification. For what God declares in Heaven he truly effects on earth.

Here is the heart of Newman's theology of salvation. Here is what made him rejoice—God himself living in our hearts. He claimed that:

> Whatever blessings in detail we ascribe to justification, are ascribed in Scripture to this sacred indwelling. For instance, is justification *remission of sins?* The gift of the Spirit conveys it, as is evident from the Scripture doctrine about baptism: "One baptism for the remission of sins." Is justification *adoption* into the family of God? In like manner the Spirit is expressly called the Spirit of adoption, "the Spirit whereby we cry, Abba, Father." Is justification *reconciliation* with God? St. Paul says, "Jesus Christ is in you, unless ye be reprobates." Is justification *life?* The same apostle says, "Christ liveth in me." Is justification given to *faith?* He also prays "that Christ may dwell in" Christians' "hearts by faith." Does justification lead to holy *obedience?* Our Lord assures us that "he that abideth in him and he in him, the same bringeth forth much fruit." Is it through justification that we rejoice *in hope of the glory* of God? In like manner "Christ in us" is said to be "the hope of glory." Christ then is our righteousness by dwelling in us by the Spirit; he justifies us by entering into us, he continues to justify us by remaining in us. *This* is really and truly our justification, not faith, not holiness, not (much less) a mere imputation; but through God's mercy the very Presence of Christ.[8]

So the God who declares the soul justified, is the same God who also inhabits the soul. And the God who inhabits the soul is the God who was made man and who died for our sins and rose again for our justification.

Protestants may accuse Newman of making regeneration a part of justification, but they cannot deny the beauty, the spiritual power of his doctrine.

The place of baptism and faith as instruments of justification. The instrumental cause of justification is the means by which, or the channel through which, God actually achieves the justification of the sinner. Roman Catholics had traditionally spoken of baptism as the instrument through which grace was infused by the Spirit into the soul to achieve justification. Protestants had spoken of saving faith in the hearts of the sinners, by which union with Christ and therefore justification were achieved.

Newman accepted the statement of the eleventh Article that "we are justified by *faith only*" and the words from the Homily of the Passion for Good Friday that "the only mean and instrument of salvation required on our part is faith, that is to say, a sure trust and confidence in the mercies of God." He argued that true faith, living faith, could only be found in a heart which loved God and man. So faith as the "only mean and instrument" is to be understood as the sole mean in contrast to other graces—e.g., hope, love and faithfulness. A further clarification is necessary: it is the sole *internal* instrument, not the sole instrument of any kind.

Newman had a high view of the sacraments, and it is not surprising to find him asserting that baptism is the *external* instrument. "Baptism might be the hand of the giver and faith the hand of the receiver"; and "faith secures to the soul continually those gifts which baptism primarily conveys."

We must note that Newman was addressing himself to a situation in which infant baptism was the norm. So he could say:

> Faith, then, being the appointed representative of baptism, derives its authority and virtue from that which it represents. It is justifying because of baptism; it is the faith of the baptized, of the regenerate, that is, of the justified.[9]

Thus faith is always, when considered as an instrument, secondary to baptism. Newman actually believed that this was also true with respect to adult conversion to Christianity. He quoted such texts as "Be baptized every one of you for the remission of sins" (Acts 2:38) and noted the close connection in the New Testament between baptism and forgiveness of sins. Newman held that faith was different in quality before and after baptism, for baptism changed faith from a condition into an instrument, from a "mere forerunner into its accredited representative." Faith "is renewed in knowledge when Christ is imparted as a Spirit." Newman saw proof of this power in the description of the faith of the jailer in Acts.

Newman was ready to accept that "by faith alone" is a "lively mode of speech [figurative] for saying that we are justified neither by faith, nor by works, but by God only." He found this usage in Melanchthon, the Homilies, Bishop Bull and others, but he believed that "it was more adapted for the schools, than for the taste of a people like the English at the present day."

Here is Newman's summary of the relationship between faith, the sacraments, love and obedience:

> Reserving to baptism our new birth, and to the Eucharist the ultimate springs of the new life, and to love what may be called its plastic power, and to obedience its being the atmosphere in which faith breathes, still the divinity appointed or (in other words) the mysterious virtue of faith remains. It alone coalesces with the sacraments, brings them into effect, dissolves (as it were) their outward case, and through them unites the soul to God.[10]

So faith both develops and sanctifies other graces, like salt in food or incense on sacrifices.

Newman was thus able to reconcile the seeming differences between the teaching of St. Paul and St. James. His view was that "Justification comes *through* the sacraments; is received by faith; consists in God's inward presence and lives in obedience."[11]

Newman reissued his lectures in 1874 when he was a respected Roman Catholic. The material is precisely the same, except for the addition of a new preface of about a thousand words and fourteen brief notes placed in square brackets at the bottom of appropriate pages (e.g., pages 31, 73, 101, etc.).

In the preface, written at the Oratory in Birmingham, he stated: "Unless the author held in substance in 1874 what he published in 1838 he would not at this time be reprinting what he wrote as an Anglican; certainly not with so little added by way of safeguard."

The "little . . . by way of safeguard" primarily concerned two views which he had expressed in 1838 and 1840 as being at variance with traditional Roman Catholicism and which he now realized (looking at the matter from within rather than from without) were not truly at variance. First, he had given the impression that there was more than one *formal* cause of the justified state. Now he admitted that there was one formal cause and that was the inward, divine gift. However, he placed himself on the side of the early Fathers by claiming that he had not written with the precision of the logicians and schoolmen but in the orthodox and yet less precise language of men such as Athanasius and Augustine. Therefore, what he had written was not truly at variance with Tridentine Catholicism. Secondly, he had allowed that one possible *formal* cause was the presence of the Lord in the soul of man. His defense here was to claim that he wrote in the same way as did the great mystical theologian, Dominikus Schramm (1722-1797) of Bavaria. Again, he was not attempting to be a logician but a follower of the early Fathers, and he had thus not been in error.

It is obvious that Newman was at variance only with the scholastic exposition of Tridentine Catholicism, because his mind did not easily work in the logical categories of scholasticism but in the warm devotional categories of the Fathers and mystics. This feature of his thought began in his Anglican period.

Michael Schmaus

In *Justification and the Last Things* (1977) Schmaus presents an attractive and at times sophisticated explanation of the official Roman Catholic teaching on justification. He finds the dogma of the Council of Trent satisfactory, except at a few points where he is ready to make criticism.

It perhaps needs emphasizing that while he makes much use of Scripture, he does so under the umbrella of a definition of justification as the process of making just or righteous. There is no exegesis of the New Testament passages in which justification is the central or subsidiary theme (e.g., from Romans or Galatians). The traditional medieval understanding of *justificare* as "to make righteous/just" is taken for granted. No attempt is made to explain the weight of biblical scholarship which sees the forensic meaning as prominent in the New Testament usage of *dikaioō*. In other words, he works from the definition given at Trent: "Justification is not only the remission of sins, but sanctification and renovation of the interior man through the voluntary reception of grace and gifts, whereby a man becomes just instead of unjust and a friend instead of an enemy, that he may be an heir in the hope of life everlasting."

Further, though he supplies some explanation of the Aristotelian categories used at Trent he makes no effort to show what the Roman Catholic doctrine would look like if it were presented in different conceptual categories. He appears content to affirm that the theology of Trent was basically metaphysical and that the theology of the major Protestant confessions was biblical and existential in character.

Grace and freedom. He maintains that justification is only possible through divine grace, which is wholly the gift of God and in no way can be merited. In traditional terms, the "meritorious cause" is the sacrificial death and glorious resurrection of the incarnate Son of God, and the "efficient cause" is the action of the merciful God who washes and sanctifies, who pardons and purifies his people. So he can see truth in the Reformation slogan of *sola gratia* (by grace alone). The phrase expresses a legitimate concern in that it makes clear that it is God who always takes the initiative in his saving movement towards sinners. In eternity God decided on his plan of salvation; the eternal Son became man and died for the world; the Holy Spirit entered the Church and world in Christ's name to make effective what the Savior had done. Yet, while salvation proceeds wholly from grace, to say "grace alone" can be misleading. "God's initiative only reaches its goal, is only intended to reach its goal if man allows himself to be grasped by God's grace."[12] However, the process in which God takes the initiative and man freely responds defies any concise explanation. It certainly happens, but it is impossible to describe it fully or accurately.

Further, grace is given not to make sinners painfully aware of their wretchedness, but rather to release for them the potentialities inherent in becoming a child of God. Schmaus, in common with other Roman Catholic theologians, views Reformation theology as emphasizing too much the sinfulness, weakness and depravity of human nature; Schmaus and friends think especially of the stress on human depravity in the teaching of Luther's *The Bondage of the Will* (1525).

Concerning faith, Schmaus happily accepts such statements as these from the *Decree on Justification* of the Council of Trent: "Faith, unless hope and charity be added thereto, neither unites man perfectly with Christ, nor makes him a living member of his body" (chap. 7). And, "Faith is the beginning of human salvation, the foundation and root of all justification" (chap. 8). Faith, he writes, "is the first step towards Christ, no more, no less." It is also "a living force which gives birth to all the other attitudes mentioned by the Council—hope, love, repentance, confidence—and continues to support them."[13]

Faith is certainly not an activity by which the sinner makes himself worthy of justification. Rather, "faith makes one receptive to the justification effected by God." It is not faith and works but faith as the root and source of good works. Understood in this way, the traditional Roman Catholic concept of faith need not be opposed to the "by faith alone" of the Protestant Reformers, at least not if the Protestant view of faith is something like this: "faith is the total living process of unconditioned and confident self-abandonment to God and to his promise. Penance, love and hope and a ready obedience are included in the total living process."

Misunderstanding has occurred, says Schmaus, because the doctrinal expression of the *Decree* of Trent tends towards the metaphysical, whereas that of the Reformers is more existential. One important source of the theology of the Council was the teaching of Thomas Aquinas, who defined faith as an act of assent to God's revelation on the part of the intellect commanded by the will. If this may be called an intellectualist definition of faith, then that of the Protestants may be called fiducial and existential, for it emphasizes trust with commitment. Yet as Schmaus sees it, "The Council of Trent begins by giving a definition of the essence of faith only to turn itself immediately to the exercise of faith in the existential order."[14] That is, beginning from an intellectualistic view of faith, it then describes how faith expresses itself through love and hope in the Christian life in the process of justification or being made righteous. In contrast, the Protestant explanation of faith starts with the very exercise of faith itself; and starting there, it is impossible to see how faith could actually be exercised without the other elements of faithfulness, love, obedience and hope being present. Perhaps the bishops at Trent were aware of the dangers if the Protestant doctrine of *sola fide* were interpreted metaphysically (the normal Roman Catholic way of interpreting it?) instead of being placed and set within a dynamic, existential framework of reference.

Grace as the saving union with God. The purpose of grace is to bring sinners into saving union with God, into participation in the new covenant, and into the kingdom of God. This means that the Spirit indwells God's people. Schmaus does not want to encourage a static idea of union with God. He writes, " The state of justification consists in this, that it is always in the process of being created: God gives himself to man through Christ in the Spirit in an uninterrupted act. God's giving of grace to the person is a continuous act analagous to his continuing act of creation."[15] This self-communication by the tri-personal God has for its ultimate purpose the eternal union of men with God. Justification begins with the forgiveness of sins, includes interior renewal, and is completed with the ultimate redemption of the whole person in the resurrection of the body.

The forgiveness of sins by God the Father through Christ includes the remission of guilt together with the removal of the state of sinfulness (understood metaphysically) before God. This does not mean that the tendency to sin (or the disorderly inclination called concupiscence) is removed. Rather, in a metaphysical sense the forgiven person is not a sinner but a child of God. Therefore, it can be claimed only in a concrete, existential and historical sense that a Christian is simultaneously both just/righteous and a sinner. In an ontological, metaphysical sense he is only just and not a sinner.

Schmaus explains that "although the Council strongly emphasized the metaphysical reality of the forgiveness of sin, it did not reject the idea of justification which the Reformers had so much at heart. What it did deny was the statement that man is justified only through the imputation of the righteousness of Jesus Christ. The Council's definition implies that the man justified by God is declared just, but that this declaration at the same time actually creates the state of justification."[16] Justification is a sovereign act of God and is more than a mere juridical sentence, as if it were made in a human court of law. This act of God is more than a forensic act, for what it declares it puts into action. Such is the nature of the word of God Almighty! (Here it may be asked whether Schmaus is reading too much into the words of the *Decree*. Certainly what he says has become Roman Catholic teaching and, as we noted, is clearly portrayed in Newman's teaching.)

However, our author is ready to concede that the Council mistakenly emphasized the effects of the divine action (= forgiveness of sin and transformation of man) as identical with the divine act itself. It would have been better had the heavenly declaration of the Heavenly Father together with the inner renewal wrought by the Holy Spirit (two separate aspects of the one act of God) been clearly distinguished from the results of this unified act of God (the results being forgiveness and renewal).

Schmaus is also at pains to point out that much confusion has arisen in the understanding of the *Decree* by not maintaining a careful distinction between the efficient and formal causes of justification. "With regard to efficient causality," he writes, "there is no difference between the Council of Trent and Luther. . . . The difference lies in the area of formal cause. . . . If Aristotelian philosophy is regarded as an unsuitable instrument for theology, then the doctrine of formal cause is inaccessible."[17] In defending the Tridentine position Schmaus speaks of righteousness as "deriving from without" and being "so implanted in a man as to belong to him not as a possession like material goods he can dispose of according to his wishes, but as an assured gift bestowed in a continuous act of grace for which he is responsible."[18] He admits that the doctrine of a formal cause does not explain how inner renewal comes about; it only describes the metaphysical structure, stating in what it consists. Thus the precise connection between inner renewal and the forgiveness of sins was not fixed by the Council, and different theological interpretations (developing from the Aristotelian categories) are possible and have been offered.

Justification—the personal, existential aspect. In his saving communication with human beings, God brings healing. This involves a change both in a man's metaphysical essence and in his human faculties. The latter has been described in terms of the infusion of the virtues—both the theological (faith, hope and love) and the moral (wisdom, fortitude, justice and prudence). Working from this traditional base, Schmaus carefully examines the theological virtues from a biblical perspective. He says little about the moral virtues, seeing them as "powers enabling a man, in Christ and with Christ, to do justice to the demands of real-life situations in the spirit of love." The point he is making is that justification is a real making just and that this real justice may be explained in terms of the virtues as they develop in the Christian.

Schmaus also briefly explains his conviction that "the belief in the regeneration of the justified man reached its theological completion in the teaching of the seven gifts of the Spirit." These are based on the Latin text of Isaiah 11:2, which speaks of the spirit of wisdom and understanding, of counsel and fortitude, of knowledge and piety and fear of the Lord. "Today," he remarks, "there is a general acceptance by systematic theology of the ideas proposed by Aquinas: that the gifts of the Spirit effect a special interior relationship with God, preparing the heart to experience the divine impulses not as alien or threatening but as familiar and satsifying, so that he will respond to them with alacrity and joy."[19] That is, the gifts of the Spirit produce a delicate receptivity to the divine presence, so that by his leading the Christian does what is right.

But is it possible to be certain that one is justified? Schmaus is aware that the contents of the *Decree* can be interpreted both as portraying the theology of the Reformers in an unfair manner and as not emphasizing a right approach to Christian assurance. He sees the teaching of the Council as an attack upon Pharisaism, false confidence, self-reliance, self-satisfaction and the belief that a person can possess God as an object, using him like a practical possession. He is ready to concede that there is such a thing as Christian certainty of justification, but he insists that it needs to be carefully explained. "We can have no such certainty as that which we possess in our assent in faith to the truths of revelation, because in the state of justification the personal, existential element always enters in. Nor can we have the kind of certainty we have of the highest metaphysical and mathematical principles, or of things observable by the senses: the kind of certainty we have is in accordance with the object. We can, however, have the kind of certainty about justification which has its place in human relations. This certainty, termed 'moral' certainty by scholastic philosophy and theology, has its basis in human reliability and faithfulness. It is sufficient and necessary for the conduct of human life. It consists in this— that in man's moral behavior one counts on his dependability and faithfulness."[20] This kind of certainty can reach such an intensity that there is little or no room for rational doubt. We may add that Protestant teaching appears to be of a different kind and related more to the inner illumination of the Spirit than to the concept of moral certainty.

Schmaus also asks, Are there gradations in justification? If justification is only extrinsic, as Protestants maintain, then is it exactly the same in nature and intensity for every believer? If justification is also intrinsic, as Trent maintained, then although in essence the justice imparted to the soul is the same, it differs from one person to the next in grades of intensity and depth. If it is allowed that justification is a process, then there must be growth and Christians must be at different stages of the process of growth.

Another vexing question is, Can the state of justification be lost? Schmaus rightly recognizes that there is in the New Testament a tension between the indicative and the imperative of salvation. The new life given by God is certainly a gift, but it must be maintained, in some sense, by the person who receives it. The Reformers held that justification could not be lost because it was pronounced by God, as judge, concerning those whom he had elected unto eternal life from eternity. This, in Schmaus's view, is to stress the indicative so much as not to be able to sufficiently emphasize the imperative of salvation. The Council, taking the biblical emphasis on the imperative seriously, taught that justification as a state could be lost through mortal sin or through abandonment of faith. In the Tridentine teaching the idea of eternal predestination does not function as it does in Luther's or Calvin's teaching. Only those who persevere to the end and actually enter Heaven are the elect. A Christian does not cooperate with divine grace because he is one of the elect (as in Luther/Calvin), but rather, using his free will in a responsible way with God's help, he becomes one of the elect by completing the process of justification, assisted by divine grace.

The fruit of justification. Purposing to show that the person in the process of justification is called to be active not only in pursuit of personal holiness but also in the pursuit of justice in the world, Schmaus moves out from the traditional scholastic categories. He shows that the life of God in the human heart should affect personal relationships and should motivate and direct participation of the individual and the church community in the life of both natural (e.g., the family) and established (e.g., the town or city) communities to which they belong. At the level of personal encounter, there will be a practical recognition of the value and dignity of the human person. At the level of participation in human society, Schmaus follows the general principles and suggestions of Vatican II as set forth in such documents as *The Church in the Modern World* and *Religious Freedom.*

From the attempt to speak in modern terms of the involvement of the justified in the modern world, Schmaus reverts to traditional categories to explain the concept of merit. By God's help, the Christian does all kinds of good works and then is rewarded for these by the God of grace with the gift of eternal life. "Man can produce acts worthy of salvation because, and insofar as, God produces them through him. Only in the creative power of God can man be creative. In the works of a man possessed and ruled by God, the prime actor is God: and hence it is of God's own works that we say they are 'meritorious.' They participate in the value, the dignity, and the majesty of God, and are in no way impaired by the fact that God works through human weakness or that human imperfection is found in them."[21]

This view of merit is called *de condigno* (deserved merit). It "points up the fact that man is a wayfarer, always living in the present with an orientation towards the future. . . . But it is God himself who will bring man's efforts to completion" (p. 145). We may note that in this matter of merit, even when explained in the most careful way, there still appears to be a great gulf between Roman Catholic and Protestant teaching.

We are left wondering what shape and content a theology of justification would take if it were presented by Schmaus without reference to scholastic categories. What he has done is to interpret Trent in the most favorable way, bearing in mind the insights of modern biblical theology. In contrast, an author like the Brazilian Leonardo Boff seeks to state old categories in modern shape. He attempts to do this with "grace" in his stimulating *Liberating Grace* (1979) where, regrettably, he makes little use of the idea of justification.[22]

12   Tillich and Berkouwer

To say the least, there has been a scarcity of serious theological works devoted to justification written by English-speaking Protestant theologians in modern times. The reason for this great gap in English theological literature could be a general lack of interest in the topic among theologians. This itself could reflect a general feeling in the Christian community that the doctrine apparently does not have relevance for many twentieth-century Western Christians. An apparent lack of interest among systematic theologians and in the churches does not mean that there is no interest among professional students of the New Testament. There has been a sustained interest in the theology of the Apostle Paul, in the theme of righteousness/justice in the Bible, and in the letters of Paul to Galatia and Rome. It is perhaps true to say that much of this scholarly work has been produced in response to literature that comes from professors in German universities.

In Germany there has been and there is today much more interest in the theme of justification than in either Britain or the USA. This is due to three important factors: the seemingly never-ending study of the life and teaching of Martin Luther; the impact of dialectical or crisis theology (associated particularly with the name of Karl Barth); and debate or dialogue with Roman Catholics. Much of the scholarly biblical study has been done, for example, in response to questions generated by Luther studies. In the 1980s, with the advent of ecumenical, theological discussion, there are many signs in both Germany and Holland of scholars working together to bridge the gulf that has long existed between Roman Catholic and Protestant interpretations of the Bible.

Happily, in Britain and the USA we also have reached the stage where justification is beginning to be studied by groups of theologians and scholars from different backgrounds. In America a commission of

Lutheran and Roman Catholic theologians has since 1965 produced reports of its discussions in six volumes. In 1984 the last of these, devoted to justification, will be ready. This has been a long time in the making and should represent an important milestone in interconfessional dialogue. Also, the new International Roman Catholic/Anglican Theological Commission which began work in 1983 had on its agenda, as a major item, the topic of justification. So the way is open for a major breakthrough of understanding between Protestants and Catholics at a point where their differences have appeared impossible to reconcile.

In the light of these very recent developments, it is not easy to choose two examples of recent Protestant presentations of justification. Karl Barth would seem to be an obvious choice since he is so famous and his influence has been enormous. But his thought is not easy to present accurately in a short compass. Furthermore, the well-known study, *Justification: The Doctrine of Karl Barth and a Catholic Reflection* (1964) is readily available. After much thought I have chosen Gerrit Cornelius Berkouwer of Holland, most of whose works have appeared in English, and Paul Tillich of Germany, who lived the second half of his life in America.[1]

Paul Tillich

Born and educated in Germany, he was ordained in 1912 into the Evangelical Lutheran Church in Brandenburg. He was professor, first at Marburg (where he encountered existentialism through the teaching of Martin Heidegger), then at Dresden and finally at Frankfurt-am-Main. In 1933, when Hitler became Chancellor of Germany, he was removed from his post. So, at the age of forty-seven, he began a new career in America, teaching at Union Seminary, New York, until 1954. Afterwards he lectured first at Harvard and then at the University of Chicago. His *magnum opus* was his *Systematic Theology* in three volumes; many people, however, found his printed sermons the easiest way to appreciate what he was seeking to say.[2]

Tillich was both a philosopher and a theologian. He made use of existentialist philosophy and was committed to the Christian religion. In conscious opposition to the method of Karl Barth, which presented theology in terms of a movement from God to man, Tillich began with man in his cultural setting in the Western world. He believed that Barth's method was to present God throwing a stone from Heaven that no one was able to catch. A better method, he thought, was to begin with the questions being asked by Western human beings and then to show how, in the Christian revelation, there was an answer. This is the method of correlation, and it involves the recognition that the way the question is posed and the way the answer from divine revelation is stated are conditioned by the cultural and intellectual climate in which this process occurs. So Tillich is able to use an existentialist philosophy both to state and to answer the questions.

The norm of systematic theology. As a Lutheran, Tillich was well aware that justification by faith had been called the material norm of theology since the sixteenth century. This means that justification by faith was seen as the primary principle by which the authoritative Scriptures were to be interpreted. Justification was the hermeneutical key to open the treasures of grace in God's revelation recorded in the Bible. But is the norm of yesterday a valid norm for today?

Tillich saw the human situation around him in terms of "disruption, conflict, self-destruction, meaninglessness, and despair in all realms of life." Thus the question was not, "How may I find a merciful God and how may I receive forgiveness?" It was more like, "How may I find meaning in a meaningless world?" Therefore the norm of theology has to be "a reality in which the self-estrangement of our existence is overcome, a reality of reconciliation and reunion, of creativity, meaning and hope." And such a reality is "New Being." The concept of "New Being" was developed by Tillich from the idea of new creation in Paul's letters. Jesus the Christ is presented as the One in whom the "New Being" is seen and made available. So "the material norm of systematic theology today is the New Being in Jesus as the Christ as our ultimate concern."

This "New Being" is a pivotal concept in Tillich's system, and it is not easy to explain it in a few lines. It is God's power which liberates and transforms human beings so that they actually participate in God's new creation. As he wrote in his book *New Being* (1955): "Reconciliation, reunion, resurrection—this is the New Creation, the New Being, the New State of things. . . . A New State of things has appeared, it still appears; it is hidden and visible, it is there and it is here" (p. 24). Jesus, as the Christ, presents a perfect transparency into new creation, New Being, and he is the key to salvation.

The experience of New Being within the sphere of the Church of God can be described as the experience of the New Being as creating (= regeneration), of the New Being as paradox (= justification) and of the New Being as process (= sanctification). For Tillich, experience means "the state of being grasped by the Spiritual Presence" or the divine Spirit which is in man. The Spiritual Presence is normally made known to man through the ministry of the Word and of the sacraments. Through the Spiritual Presence the human spirit rises into successful transcendence, being delivered from the estrangement, ambiguities and irrationalities of life.

The experience of the New Being as creation (regeneration). For Tillich, the Johannine expression "new birth" and the Pauline phrase "new creation" were biblical precedents to the more abstract concept of the New Being. They all point to the same reality—that is, the event in which the divine Spirit takes hold of the personal life through the creation of faith. So regeneration must go before justification. This initial participation in the New Being is the first element in the actualization of the "Spiritual Community" (Church). Tillich commented:

If this is accepted the question is often asked: If the Spiritual Presence must grasp me and create faith in me, what can I do in order to reach such faith? I cannot force the Spirit upon myself; so what can I do but wait without acting? Sometimes this question is asked without seriousness, in an attitude of dialectical aggression, and does not really require an answer. No answer can be given to him who asks in this way, because every answer would tell him something he should do or be; it would contradict the faith for which he asks. If, however, the question—What can I do in order to experience the New Being?—is asked with existential seriousness, the answer is implied in the question, for existential seriousness is evidence of the impact of the Spiritual Presence upon an individual. He who is ultimately concerned about the state of estrangement and about the possibility of reunion with the ground and aim of his being is already in the grip of the Spiritual Presence. In this situation the question, What shall I do to receive the divine Spirit? is meaningless because the real answer is already given and any further answer would distort it.[3]

So the position is that the person who asks with "ultimate concern" should be told that the fact of his ultimate concern implies the answer: he is already under the impact and influence of the Spiritual Presence.

The experience of the New Being as paradox (justification). Tillich first gained the insight that a man is justified by grace through faith (not only as a sinner but even as a doubter) when he was a student at Halle in 1905 listening to Martin Kähler. In the light of two world wars he became painfully aware that the Protestant doctrine of justification was not readily understood even by Protestants. "The idea is strange to the man of today and even to Protestant people in the churches: indeed, as I have over and over again had the opportunity to learn, it is so strange to modern man that there is scarcely any way of making it intelligible to him." Despite this problem of communication, Tillich did seek to interpret the New Testament teaching in terms of the New Being.

Before offering his own interpretation Tillich dealt with three "semantic problems." First, the expression "justification *by faith.*" The use of it, he believed, had led to a devastating confusion. "Faith, in this phrase, has been understood as the cause of God's justifying act, which means that the moral and ritual works of Catholic teaching are replaced by the intellectual work of accepting a doctrine." So he proposed that the expression should be, "justification by grace through faith."

In the second place, the term "justification" cannot have the meaning for us that it had for Paul's time since we do not share his cultural setting. So "it should be replaced in the practice of teaching and preaching by the term 'acceptance,' in the sense that we are accepted by God, although being unacceptable according to the criteria of law ... and that we are asked to accept this acceptance." Such terminology is itself acceptable by people, he believed, for whom the Old and New Testament phrasing has lost all meaning, although there is a most serious existential meaning for them in the reality to which this phrasing points.

Thirdly, he pointed out the limitations of the expression, "forgiveness of sins" to express the paradoxical character of the experience of the New Being. One of these had to do with the picture behind the idea of forgiveness, that of the debtor and the one to whom he is in debt. In all human relations the one who forgives has the need himself to be forgiven, but with God this is not the case. Another limitation had to do with the fact that while a man forgives a particular offense (debt/sin) God forgives sin, the act of separation from God and the resistance to union with him. Thus he concluded that Paul's use of justification was a more satisfactory way of presenting the way in which the New Being is experienced, for it relates forgiveness to justice and to Christ. Further, it makes clear the unconditional character of the divine act in which God declares him who is unjust to be just.

Luther's paradox, *simul justus, simul peccator,* points to this unconditional divine declaration and highlights the truth that God accepts the undeserving. Tillich perceived in both Paul and Luther a profound psychological insight into the relationship of the sinner who knows himself to be unacceptable to God, who accepts the unacceptable. He wrote: "This surrender of one's own goodness occurs in him who accepts the divine acceptance of himself, the unacceptable. The courage to surrender one's own goodness to God is the central element in the courage of faith. In it the paradox of the New Being is experienced, the ambiguity of good and evil is conquered, unambiguous life has taken hold of man through the impact of the Spiritual Presence." Tillich also pointed to the picture of Jesus, the Crucified One. Here there is God's acceptance of the unacceptable and God's participation in man's estrangement.

Tillich set himself to answer a question which Paul and Luther had not faced and which Augustine and the Apostle John had only partially recognized. How is faith, justifying faith, related to radical doubt (the existential doubt concerning the meaning of life itself)? He wrote:

The first part of every answer to this problem must be negative: God as the truth and the source of meaning cannot be reached by intellectual work, as he cannot be reached by moral work. The question, "What can I do to overcome radical doubt and the feeling of meaninglessness?" cannot be answered, because every answer would justify the question, which implies that something can be done. But the paradox of the New Being is that nothing can be done by man who is in the situation in which he asks the question. One can only say, while rejecting the form of the questions, that the seriousness of despair in which the question is asked is itself the answer. This is in the line of Augustine's argument, that in the situation of doubt the truth from which one feels separated is present insofar as in every doubt the formal affirmation of truth is presupposed. But the analogous affirmation of meaning within meaninglessness is also related to the paradox of justification. It is the problem of the justification, not of the sinner, but of him who doubts, which has led to this solution. Since in the predicament of doubt and meaninglessness God as the source of the justifying act has disappeared, the only thing left (in which God reappears without being recognized) is the ultimate honesty of doubt and the unconditional seriousness of the despair about meaning.[4]

This is the way that Tillich believed the people of Western society could be told that they are accepted with respect to the ultimate meaning of their lives, although unacceptable in view of the doubt and meaninglessness which has taken hold of them. God is actually present to them in the seriousness of their existential despair.

The experience of the New Being as process (sanctification). Tillich expressed reservations about the Lutheran, Calvinist and Wesleyan ways of describing sanctification, even though he perceived good points in each of them. They did not speak to modern man. He proposed instead "four principles which united religious and secular traditions and which in their totality create an indefinite but yet distinguishable image of the Christian life."

(1) Increasing awareness. This is the principle "according to which man in the process of sanctification becomes increasingly aware of his actual situation and the forces struggling around him and his humanity, but also becomes aware of the answers to the questions implied in this situation." These forces include both the demonic and the divine. Such an awareness "includes sensitivity towards the demands of one's own growth, toward the hidden hopes and disappointments within others, toward the voiceless voice of a concrete situation, toward the grades of authenticity in the life of the spirit in others and oneself."[5]

(2) Increasing freedom. This is the principle of freedom from the law as commandment. It is a difficult process, and maturity in it is very rare. "Freedom from the law is the power to judge the given situation in the light of the Spiritual Presence and to decide upon adequate action, which is often in seeming contradiction to the law." Further, "mature freedom from the law implies the power of resisting the forces which try to destroy such freedom from inside the personal self and from its social surroundings."[6] The danger that this freedom may turn out to be anarchy or willfulness is overcome when the power of the Spiritual Presence is at work.

(3) Increasing relatedness. This principle acts as a balance to the second. "The principle of increasing freedom cannot be imagined

without the courage to risk a wrong decision on the basis of faith, and the principle of increasing relatedness cannot be imagined without the reuniting power of *agape* to overcome *self-seclusion* fragmentarily." Relatedness implies the awareness of others and the freedom to relate to them by overcoming one's own and their self-seclusion. But relatedness also has to be towards the Spiritutal Presence because the vertical dimension (relation to God) is needed for the horizontal dimension (relation to self and others) to be actualized and meaningful. So, "as the process of sanctification approaches a more mature self-relatedness, the individual is more spontaneous, more self-affirming, without self-elevation or self-humiliations."[7]

(4) Increasing transcendence. Sanctification is not possible, Tillich tells us, without a continuous transcendence of oneself in the direction of the ultimate—in other words, without participation in the holy. However, it is a mistake to think that this participation only occurs in the distinctly religious or churchy situation.

> The self-transcendence which belongs to the principles of sanctification is actual in every act in which the impact of the Spiritual Presence is experienced. This can be in prayer or meditation in total privacy, in the exchange of Spiritual experiences with others, in communications on a secular basis, in the experience of creative works of man's spirit, in the midst of labour or rest, in private counseling, in church services. It is like the breathing-in of another air, an elevation above average existence. It is the most important thing in the process of Spiritual maturity. Perhaps one can say that with increasing maturity in the process of sanctification the transcendence becomes more definite and its expressions more indefinite. Participation in communal devotion may decrease and the religious symbols connected with it may become less important, while the state of being ultimately concerned may become more manifest and the devotion to the ground and aim of our being more intensive.[8]

Tillich believed that the awareness of the need for the experience of transcendence was a characteristic of Western society after the Second World War. People looked to Christianity for concrete symbols of self-transcendence.

Tillich did not think that perfection was possible in the life of the Christian. He recognized that there would always be ups and downs, but there could be and should be movement towards maturity.

We must recognize that Tillich's proposals on justification and sanctification are part of a total systematic presentation. These particular proposals stand or fall, not on their own merit alone, but on the merit of the foundations of the system as a whole—and these are too complex to study here.[9] However, if we judge that his theological system is, in the last analysis, a failure, it is still possible to claim that some of his warnings and suggestions have value. In particular, he causes us to ask these questions: Can justification, presented in the Protestant Confessions and tradition as heavily forensic, ever be a powerful symbol for Western Christian people again? Are we more concerned by life's meaninglessness than by a consciousness of sinning against God, the judge? Is the model of acceptance a better model than that of justification? These are questions worth pondering.

G. C. Berkouwer

Berkouwer is a good example of a modern-day Calvinist theologian.[10] He became professor of dogmatics at the Free University of Amsterdam at the end of the Second World War and introduced a new mood into the theology of the Reformed Church. He certainly taught his theology as a faithful son of his denomination and as one who heartily accepted its confessions of faith *(Heidelberg Catechism, Belgic Confession* and the *Canons of Dort)*. This does not mean that he did his theology in a seventeenth-century manner. He greatly admired Calvin, and, like the reformer of Geneva, his theology is composed of biblical exegesis, explanation of the confessional heritage, answering contemporary questions and seeking to be faithful to Christ.

This methodology is seen in his *Studies in Dogmatics* (eighteen volumes). Three volumes are relevant to our inquiry. They are *Faith and Justification* (Dutch 1949, English 1954), *Faith and Sanctification* (1949, 1952) and *Faith and Perseverance* (1949, 1958). As one who stood in a particular dogmatic tradition, Berkouwer was always conscious of particular questions which had exercised the minds of the major Reformed/Lutheran dogmaticians of Europe in days past. So it is not surprising that his book on justification begins with a discussion of the *ordo salutis.*

The "ordo salutis." Aware of modern theology's criticisms of attempts to produce an *ordo salutis,* Berkouwer accepted much of the censure but also attempted to make a positive suggestion. He knew that "the origin of the *ordo salutis* was closely connected with a virulent defense of the gospel. . . . The analysis of the application of salvation to man was part of a criticism of those who underestimated the influences of sin on the human soul and who minimized the perversion of human nature."[11] He recognized that the *order* had often overshadowed the *salvation,* and so he could write: "Though it may satisfy an appetite for logical construction, the order of salvation can be given no independent significance." It had to be related to genuine Christian piety.

He admired the approach of Calvin and commended the expression "way of salvation" as more biblical than "order." "Sometimes generations of Christians have lost the joy of the gospel by having gone amiss on the *way of salvation.* This is why it is perpetually necessary for the Church to reflect on . . . the way of salvation. The purpose of her reflection is not to refine and praise the logical systematization. It is to cut off every way in which Christ is not confessed exclusively as *the Way.*"[12] Therefore his approach to justification and sanctification and all aspects of soteriology is determined by his desire to make the way of salvation true to Christ and as clear as possible. In effect this means he has little or no discussion, in the traditional sense, of the *ordo salutis* in logical terms.

The *"sola fide"* and *"sola gratia."* Berkouwer's examination of the confessional documents of his denomination shows that he accepted wholeheartedly their teaching on justification. "A single theme plays through all three documents, *The Belgic Confession, The Heidelberg Catechism* and *The Canons of Dort*—the theme of *sola fide.* And this is the heart of the Reformed confession. The various and varied expressions are religiously simple and transparent. The fathers understood that justification through faith alone was the confession preeminent, the confession *sine qua non.*"[13] And to confess *sola fide* is also to confess *sola gratia.*

But were the basic Lutheran confessions in agreement with the Reformed? Did Luther teach a different approach or did Melanchthon confuse the matter? Berkouwer believed that in confession of *sola fide,* the two traditions of the Reformation in their early years were one. Thus he rejected the contention (often made on the Continent in the 1930s and 1940s) that Lutheran doctrine is basically synthetic and Calvinist belief is analytical concerning justification by faith. Synthetic justification was used to describe the view that justification is a declarative judgment of God as judge, made solely on the basis of Christ's saving work, and made only to faith. In contrast, analytical justification was used to describe the view that the declarative judgment of God was made primarily on the basis that the believer would be faithful to the end, as he lived as a Christian with the aid of the grace of God. Berkouwer held that the *Augsburg Confession* and the *Apology* for it were at one in teaching a common doctrine of justification *sola fide* and *sola gratia;* this teaching in no way made sanctification a condition of justification.

The Protestant confession of *sola fide* is a warning sign along the path of the history of the Church. But *sola fide*

carries no guarantee against the deceits of the human heart. No formula is a security for the glory of God. *Sola fide* makes sense only in the act of true faith. But the confessions of the Reformation are plain. They tell of grace without the works of the law; they witness against the glory, the elevation, and the trustworthiness of man. They whisper of the comfort of God's redemption, but in such a way as to suggest the danger of making man's comfort the *alpha* and *omega* of Christianity. The warning is needed, for we would undoubtedly enjoy making of the doctrine of justification a projection of our own wishes and desires, a postulate of our own distress. But *sola fide* points the other way, towards God's elective love in Jesus Christ who takes priority over all human desires. This is why *sola fide* is theocentric, and *therefore* soteriological. For the grace of God *that bringeth salvation* has appeared to all men (Titus 2:11). This description of grace concludes with the expectation of the *glorious* appearance of our *great* God and Savior Jesus Christ (Titus 2:13). *Sola fide! Soli Deo Gloria!*[14]

Berkouwer saw a beautiful correspondence between the comfort of the *sola fide* and the objectivity of the *Soli Deo Gloria.* They belong together, as they were united in the life of Abraham: "He did not waver through unbelief regarding the promise of God, but was strengthened in his faith and gave glory to God" (Rom. 4:20).

The Reformation and an overdependence upon the letters of Paul? Berkouwer faced the old question, "Did the Reformers establish a specifically Pauline gospel?" He admitted that "it is undeniable . . . that Paul's letters played a peculiarly significant role in the Reformation. In reading the sermons of the Reformation era one almost hears the voice of St. Paul."[15] Yet he maintained that the Reformation was concerned with the whole of Scripture, but the particular conditions of the Church in Europe in the early sixteenth century made the teaching of Paul a key by which to unlock the treasures in the rest of Scripture. He repeated the common Protestant view that there is a remarkable correspondence "between Paul's struggle against Judaism in both its gross and its refined work-righteousness and the Reformation struggle against human merit." He went on to affirm that "it was the gospel that reached its climax in Paul's preaching which roused itself in the Reformation and shook off the shackles of the contrition and attrition technique, the system of penance, and the idea of merit which kept it bound during much of the Middle Ages."[16] But the doctrine of *sola fide* and *sola gratia* is not merely Pauline and is not one-sided. It is presupposed and taught throughout all the New Testament. If Luther did sometimes talk as though Paul's letters were the only genuine parts of the New Testament, it has to be remembered that Calvin preached through all the books of the Bible, and the churches of the Reformation were committed to all the Scriptures and to the wholeness of the gospel of grace in all the parts.

Paul's sharp antithesis of righteousness through faith and not by works must be maintained but has been misunderstood. Faith can never be a work, a kind of attitude or mental state which I bring to God in contrast to external achievements in terms of good works. It is the absence of anything meritorious in myself as I look to the cross of Christ. It is *fiducia,* trusting faith. And it is not the ground of justification but the instrument (the channel or means) of justification. The instrumental function of faith is to point and look to Christ alone.

To think of faith as a kind of subjective righteousness produced in me by the external righteousness of Christ is also to misunderstand.

The "faith" reckoned for righteousness (Gen. 15:6) to which Paul (Rom. 4:3, 9, 22) makes reference is not a subjective righteousness. "It was reckoned unto him for righteousness" is an abbreviation meaning that God reckons his own righteousness (poured out in Christ) to the person who looks to him in faith and on that basis pardons and accepts him. "We are prohibited from abstracting a 'subjective righteousness' from the imputed righteousness of Christ, since it is precisely his righteousness with which faith is concerned. Imputation of the righteousness of Christ does not mean that God takes due note of and makes proper response to a subjective righteousness possessed by Abraham and all believers. It is the act of his grace in Christ."[17]

Only in the forensic concept of justification, taught by Paul and set out in the Protestant confessions, does the *sola fide/sola gratia* theme find its purest expression. Therefore the synthetic character of justification must be emphasized as the authentic approach. In the mid-1940s Berkouwer was conscious of powerful attempts to advance the analytical understanding, and he felt obliged to emphasize the traditional, Reformed, synthetic understanding. In its defense and commendation of the forensic understanding, the Reformation pointed mankind to the free grace of God and thereby did not endanger but rescued commitment to holy living from misunderstanding and neglect. (To the relation of justification and sanctification we shall return below.)

Possible challenges to the "sola fide" understanding. Does not Scripture teach that we shall be judged according to our works? Berkouwer replied in the affirmative but went on to make a distinction between "works of the law" and "works of faith." He saw "works" as giving form to faith in real-life situations. The actual doing of the will of God is proof that faith is genuine. So judgment according to works is not an analytical ethical judgment but an infallible perception of works in their relation to faith. As the Protestant confessions declare, good works arise from faith and aim at the glory of God. Thus it is only the works of the law and not the works of faith which actually threaten the *sola fide* understanding of salvation. True faith is related to freedom; and freedom is related to the guidance and fruit of the Spirit.

Secondly, does not Scripture teach that there will be a future reward for works done here on earth? Berkouwer faced this question very conscious of traditional Protestant opposition to the Roman Catholic doctrine of merit and reward. Perhaps it may be said that he was so wrapped up in this traditional battle that his answer here was less convincing than with regard to judgment according to works. He held that the parable of the workers in the vineyard (Matt. 20:1-16) illuminated the relation of faith and rewards. The generosity of God, as here illustrated, cannot be fitted into any strict system of justice and merit. Thus all understanding of merit and reward must be conditioned by the priority of God's grace and mercy. Talk of merit and reward can suggest that God has an obligation to deliver compensation for human claims. At this point the gospel of grace is no more. He quoted Calvin with approval: "It appears beyond all doubt that the Lord rewards the works of believers with those blessings which he had already given them before their works were thought of, and while he had no reason for his beneficence but his own mercy" (*Institutes*, III.18.2.).

Rewards do not enter as a new phenomenon alongside divine mercy, for it is through God's mercy that rewards make sense. "The confession of God's mercy is so broad and profound that it does not cramp the Christian hope for reward: it establishes it and gives it meaning. Rewards and *sola fide—sola gratia* go well together. It is he who has understood the significance of *sola fide* who is able to speak meaningfully of the relation between the works of faith and reward: he is guarded against the deceit of the human heart which threatens ever to substitute for this relation, grounded in God's mercy, a correlation arranged outside the divine mercy, and through which the religion of faith in God's sovereign grace is seriously endangered."[18] This is fine, but Berkouwer did not really face the question as to whether Christians are given greater or less rewards, no rewards or some rewards, insofar as they have allowed the divine mercy to work in and through them.

Thirdly, is it not the case that St. James teaches the doctrine of justification by works and not by faith? There is no need for us to follow Berkouwer's exegesis of James 2, for he deals with it in a familiar Protestant manner. He concludes by stating: "James' point is this—true faith is not dead, empty or fruitless. It is experienced in the daily reality of life. Be James's letter directed against whom it may, it is not aimed at Paul." He continued, "That this whole James vs. Paul affair could have arisen at all is only ascribable to a failure to distinguish between works of the law and the works of faith."[19] He regretted Luther's widely publicized rejection of the letter of James and claimed that rightly understood this letter is a powerful call to true faith which results in works of faith.

Justification and sanctification. To establish the right connection between justification and sanctification is very important, claimed Berkouwer. It is not a transition from theory to practice or from the sphere of faith to that of the practicalities of reality. "The moment sanctification is ejected from the temple of faith, and hence of justification, that moment justification by faith has become an initial stage on the pilgrim's journey, a supply-station which later becomes a pleasant memory!"[20] The real connection between the two is *sola fide*. This will become clear as we note how Berkouwer understood sanctification.

The people of Israel may be described both as being sanctified by God and therefore to be sanctified. The relation between God's sanctification of Israel and the self-sanctification of Israel is not one of competition or of cooperation. It is that of the divine initiative, setting apart and calling for the people to live as those set apart, followed by the response of Israel (a response always dependent on divine grace). This is a harmonious correlation and is also seen in the New Testament. The sanctification of the Church and of the believer are an implication of the sanctification that is already a fact in Christ by God's mercy. *He* is our sanctification. Berkouwer opposed the attempt to state that in the relation of "already sanctified in Christ" and "yet to be sanctified" there is an antinomy (a paradox or contradiction). The possibility of an antinomy is dispelled by the simple fact that the sanctification of the believer is a corollary of his faith. Self-sanctification is the response of the man of faith to the call of God. It is not the cooperation of the believer with God but the continuing obedience of faith to the word of God. Rightly understood, *sola fide* does not result in antinomianism—"let us sin that grace may abound"—but in joyful submission to the will of God. *Sola fide* is the glue that binds together sanctification and justification. It is also that which challenges the concept of grace, merit and reward which is found in the decrees and canons of the Council of Trent.

   The nature of sanctification. After a fair statement of John Wesley's teaching on perfection and a commendation of his insistence on the *sola fide* in justification, Berkouwer found his doctrine of perfectionism to have illicit relations with synergism (= the "working together" of the human will and the grace of God) and with nomism (= legal rigorism). Further, Wesley (and all perfectionists) misunderstood the significance of *sole fide* for the whole of the Christian life and experience. Berkouwer accepted the teaching of the *Heidelberg Catechism* at Day 44. The answer to the question, "Can those who are converted to God perfectly keep the commands?" is, "No; but even the holiest men, while in this life, have only small beginnings of this obedience; yet so, that with a sincere resolution they begin to live, not only according to some, but all the commands of God." He held that this position was the right way of understanding Romans 7:14-25, always a critical passage in the discussion of sin in the heart of the believer. The believer is constantly in a battle against sin, and this battle has no ending in this life. To see God more clearly is to see one's sin more clearly. "To speak of the Church is to speak of the struggle to remain children of God in communion with him and to live gratefully in virtue of the forgiveness of sins. The life of sanctification proceeds in weakness, temptation and exposure to the powers of darkness. . . . Perfectionism is a premature seizure of the glory that will be: an anticipation leading irrevocably to nomism."[21]

   Much of Berkouwer's discussion of the origin and progress of sanctification is done in dialogue with the views of his illustrious predecessors Abraham Kuyper (1837-1920) and Hermann Bavinck (1854-1921). So it is not always very helpful or illuminating for the Anglo-Saxon reader. But Berkouwer is insistent that "any view of regeneration, faith, and sanctification, must be weighed and tested by the criterion of whether it does justice to the forgiveness of sins as the only ground and source of sanctification."[22] He saw this truth clearly written into the *Belgic Confession* (Article 24), which states that it is faith which regenerates man and causes him to live a new life. *Sola fide* is central in all thinking about justification, regeneration (birth from above) and sanctification (the progress in love of God and man).

"Process" suggests an evolutionary development, and sanctification is not like that. "Progress" also is not a perfect word, for the "progress" or "process" or sanctification is to be compared with no other progress or process, says Berkouwer. So often analogies and metaphors have done violence to its special, unique character. "For progress in sanctification never meant working out one's own salvation under one's own auspices; on the contrary, it meant working out one's own salvation with a rising sense of dependence on God's grace."[23] The latter is increased, said Berkouwer, by a right understanding and use of both the "imitation of Christ" and the "holy law of God"—themes which he carefully expounds.

"Sola fide" and the perseverance of the saints. We cannot delve deeply into Berkouwer's study of perseverance, except to note that he has an illuminating study of the controversy of Calvinists with Remonstrants (Arminians), Roman Catholics, and Lutherans, and that the position he adopts is based on his confessions of faith. But he is insistent that *sola fide* is significant for the understanding of perseverance. "One can tread the road of perseverance only in faith, and the doctrine of perseverance is possible only in this faith. That is because this faith is oriented to the *faithfulness of God,* apart from which any talk about our perseverance becomes mere gibberish. Indeed, the doctrine of perseverance finds its only possibility and meaning in the faithfulness of God."[24]

It is probably true to claim that Berkouwer shows the clearest insight of any recent theologian into the function of *sola fide* in salvation. For this reason alone he is worth reading carefully. In that his exposition is so faithful to the Reformed confessions (interpreted according to the intention of their original authors) his writings tend to make the Reformed faith come alive for those who belong to its tradition rather than making converts to it. If Barth may be called an original thinker, Berkouwer may be called an interpreter of the original thinking of the fathers of the Calvinistic churches.

13 Conclusion

What is likely to happen in the near future is a general consensus among biblical scholars of all kinds as to the meaning of righteousness and justification in the Bible, especially in the Pauline letters. In the light of centuries of disagreement this will be a great step forward. It will not, however, be the end of the road. Exegesis, we recall, is only the first part of hermeneutics!

As Christians living in the latter part of the twentieth century, we have to ask whether we can see how what Paul taught the Galatian and Roman churches nineteen centuries ago as "Word of God" can also for us today be "Word of God." The oft-quoted observation of Tillich that justification by faith is so strange to modern man that there is scarcely any way of making it intelligible to him must be noted. We have to ask ourselves: What form should the message of justification take today so that the meaning intended (by the Holy Spirit through Paul) originally as Word of God is the meaning conveyed by us today? Obviously if we simply translate the findings of modern biblical theology into modern language, we are not interpreting. People are going to read their own understanding of law, justice, law courts and so on into the words we use. Thereby they will probably miss the meaning. Is it possible, we may also ask, to develop a forensic concept of righteousness/justification today without someone telling us that it is a legal fiction? Is there a way of doing it which does not leave the impression that justification is "just as if I had never sinned"? Is there a way of presenting it which goes further than ideas of "acquittal" (= "case dismissed" or "not guilty") and which truly leads into the richer idea of "judged to be, and actually set in, a right relationship with God"? I have met little serious discussion of such matters.

Obviously any teaching about justification has to be closely connected with our estimate of Jesus Christ—his person and his work. It may be suggested here that the doctrine of justification by faith has lost ground (and become unintelligible?) in the churches partly because it has often been tightly bound to a penal, substitutionary doctrine of the atonement (with the emphasis on *penal*). Many Christians find it hard to accept this particular theory, preferring some other—e.g., Christ as victor over death, sin, Satan—or holding to several theories. The point is that if justification is inextricably tied to one particular theory of the atonement, then it can only be a viable way of talking about our relationship to God for those who find that theory satisfying or compelling.

Also, we may note, explanations of justification have to be closely integrated into our understanding of what is the good news, the gospel of God. Sometimes, regrettably, justification is presented as if it were the actual good news instead of the explanation of why the good news is the power of God unto salvation. Preachers call upon people to "get right with God" in much the same way as they tell people "You must be born again." The fact of the matter is, of course, that no one can himself set his relationship with God right, and no one can cause the divine Spirit to enter his heart. The gospel is about Jesus, the Christ, Savior and Lord, and about the kingdom of God. Justification is the explanation of God's saving activity which makes the gospel into good news.

The meaning of sanctification in the Bible is much less a problem than righteousness. Here we may say that there is a general consensus in the scholarly world. There is division of opinion, though, in the interpretation of the theme for today—in particular over the question of "the second blessing" and related points. But this debate assumes that God's call to all Christians is that they grow in genuine love for God and for their fellow human beings. Here it is necessary to state that sanctification has to be closely related to our estimate of Christ, to the way in which we understand and proclaim the good news, and finally and especially to the work of the Holy Spirit in the Church and individual.

My own view is that if we are to continue to use the concepts of justification and sanctification, we need to present them alongside each other as two complementary metaphors—or better, two contemporary theological models. By model I mean an illustrative analogy. A model can be simple—e.g., God as King, judge, Father—or complex—e.g., God as Trinity. A model is a thought-pattern which functions in a specific way, asking us to focus on one area of reality (relationship with God) by thinking about it in terms of another area of reality (a human situation or relationship). Justification connects to our relationship with God and is based on the word of the judge in the Jewish law court; sanctification deals with our standing on God's side and is based on the principle of holiness in the Temple of Jerusalem.

Instead of speaking of justification followed by sanctification, or justification expressed in sanctification, or justification including sanctification, I suggest that we see justification and sanctification as complementary models whose truth should not be pressed into a logical or chronological relationship. Each of the two can stand on its own, but the two together give a more rounded picture of our relationship with God.

Justification

This pictures God as judge declaring that the believer is in a right relationship with himself (who is also Creator, Savior and Father). The judge makes such a declaration because of (a) what he as Savior has done for the human race, and (b) the fact that the believer comes to him only as believer, offering no self-justification or excuses for sin, but longing only for divine mercy. In terms of trinitarian belief we may say that God the Father declares the sinner to be in a right relationship with himself because he judges the sinner as believer to be united to the incarnate Son (who died and rose again for sinners), and because the sinner has been brought to such belief through the ministry of the Holy Spirit in the world. The meaning may be set out in four statements:

> The way of self-justification cannot ultimately be successful.
> God's justification is the only sure way of justification for sinners.
> God's justification in and through Christ alone is wholly free, and therefore only faith can receive it.
> God's justification brings inner freedom from the need for self-justification and releases the believer to love the neighbor for the sake of Christ.

This needs a little expansion.

One way of seeing the nature and effects of sin in human beings is in terms of the principle of self-justification. Have you noticed how often human beings engage in self-justification? A child will justify itself to his mother or teacher because he or she hates to be blamed—whether guilty or not guilty. A man or woman will use many words each day justifying himself, his existence, his actions, his past life and his general approach to life. Sometimes strict justice requires some self-justification—e.g., when talking to one's psychiatrist or doctor. But most of the time self-justification is necessary only for the sake of the human ego and identity—in order that he or she may feel accepted by others in the society in which he lives and works. Further, the craving for self-justification often leads to acute anxiety—a common problem in the Western world.

Religious people are not exempt from the tendency to self-justification and the anxiety this can cause. To believe in God does not of itself bring relief from this syndrome. So many Christian people do really believe that their good acts of kindness and concern for others commend their persons to God. They really believe that their regular attendance at worship and/or their financial support of the church (understood as building or people), their support of good causes, their readiness to help people in all kinds of need and much other activity beside, make them, however partially, acceptable to God. They think that their service to others places them in a right relationship with their Creator. Their service for others is not their problem! It is the belief that such service contributes to their justification. A key phrase in the story of the Pharisee and tax-collector is that the former was "willing to justify himself."

The point is that before God the judge there is no possible justification through presenting who I am and what I have achieved. The person who truly believes is the person who does not even find the willingness (within his faith) to present any self-justification to God. This is not to say that the Christian will not be tempted or will not ever lapse into the offering of his achievements to God in terms of self-justification. Rather, it is to say that when the Christian is motivated by genuine faith he will offer absolutely nothing to God but instead will rely entirely on what God offers him in Christ.

God justifies the ungodly and the unrighteous, for only such can be justified. Those who are whole, or think themselves whole, have no immediate need of a physician, said Jesus. Faith cannot arise in the heart of the person who persists in self-justification. Faith is the absence of self-justification, or at least the recognition that self-justification will not avail with Almighty God. To believe in him is to trust wholly in him as the God of mercy.

It was the principle of self-justification in the leaders of Judaism that forced Jesus onto the cross of Calvary on that dark Friday. They needed to prove that they were in the right, that they had the right interpretation of the Hebrew Bible, that they expected to be justified at the last day on account of their adherence to the Law of Moses. Jesus, we may say, died to absorb their and our self-justification into God's mercy without in any way impairing God's justice. He covered it with his cleansing blood. God vindicated him as the Just One, as the One who did not deserve to die but who died for others and who died in our place. God justified Jesus by the resurrection from the dead. In his vindication and justification of Jesus, God acted justly; and because Jesus died and rose as the Second Adam, the Representative Man, God made full provision in him to justify all those who would be united to this same Jesus in faith by the Holy Spirit.

God's clear verdict of justification satisfies the craving of the human heart for justification. The declaratory word of the Lord resounds in the hearts of those who believe, telling them that they *are* accepted, they *do* belong, they *have* meaning, and they *are* in a right relationship with their Creator and Redeemer. In Christ they are justified, and so there is no further need for any more self-justification before God or the world. They *are* free, set free from the bondage of the need for self-justification, in order to be able to serve others gladly and lovingly without wanting or desiring any recognition or reward. The word of the Lord who is judge is a powerful and efficacious word, for what it declares it also creates in the human heart.

It is at this point that the model of justification ceases to function as far as this life on earth is concerned (and so leaves open the use of other models to describe the Christian life). It does, however, return to tell what happens at the last day, for the declaration of a right relationship now is made in anticipation of that declaration being made at the last Great Assize. Thus justification is also a word of hope.

Sanctification

The basic picture here is of the Jerusalem Temple filled with worshipers set apart for God. We see the Lord in his eternal purity and apartness separating a people from the world, in order that they should draw near to him in worship and reflect his purity. "Be holy, for I am holy," says the Lord. In terms of trinitarian belief, we may say that God the Father calls and sets apart a people and puts them on his side. He does this through the work of the incarnate Son and by the ministry of the Holy Spirit. The meaning may be set out in four statements.

> The way of self-sanctification cannot ultimately be successful.
> God's sanctification is the only sure way of sanctification.
> God's sanctification in and through Christ is wholly free, and only faith can receive it.
> God's sanctification of our lives in space-time by the Holy Spirit requires the obedience of faith, dedication and commitment.

This needs a little expansion.

Self-sanctification is perhaps less common in the West than it was; it is, however, no less real. In those parts of the world where Buddhism, Hinduism and Islam are dominant or prominent, the principle of self-sanctification is a common feature of religious practice. Much the same was true, we are told, in the Christian world in the medieval centuries. Religious people engage in self-sanctification when they work on the assumption that their religious duties—e.g., fasting, prayers, bodily discipline—can actually make them holy and thereby set them on God's side. Contemporary Christians engage in it when they think that because, for example, they read the Bible and pray every day they are thereby in some sense holy in God's sight and estimation.

God has provided complete sanctification in the incarnate Son, Jesus Christ. He is the One who was, is, and will be forever entirely consecrated to and set apart for God. Since he is our representative at the Father's side, having first purged our sin, we are sanctified in him. In him we sit at the right hand of the Father in Heaven. Therefore, through him we offer our sacrifice of praise and thanksgiving to the Father. Further, the Holy Spirit, bearing the name and characteristics

of the exalted Jesus, actually works within us to make us in heart and
life like Christ. Thus we are sanctified in Christ by the Father, and we
are being sanctified by the Holy Spirit for the glory of the Father. The
latter process is identical in principle but different in operation in the
different personalities who by grace make up "the temple of the Holy
Spirit," "the household of faith," "the body of Christ" and "the church
of God."

Sanctification is a fuller description of the Christian's relationship
to God than justification, for it not only implies but also relates explicitly to the moral life of the believing community. And again it has
reference to the last day, for on that occasion the Church of God will be
presented as sanctified by Christ through the Holy Spirit.

Epilogue

It would be possible to describe that which God achieves through the
gospel without reference to justification and sanctification. Other models could be used to highlight the position of the believer in relation to
his Creator and Redeemer. There is the Pauline theme of reconciliation
which has all kinds of possibilities for being a powerful contemporary
theological model. Then there are the various Johannine pictures—
e.g., the vine and the branches—and the general theme in the Gospels
of forgiveness or remission of sin.

In Protestant theology over the centuries, the basic model of
justification has been enriched or expanded by incorporation into it of
other models—e.g., of forgiveness and adoption. Likewise, the model
of sanctification has been expanded or modified by the incorporation of
such models as "born of God" and "the leading of the Spirit." This is a
viable method as long as we realize what we are doing and why.

I tend to think of the various theologies of the New Testament—
the Matthean, Markan, Lukan, Johannine, Pauline, Petrine, etc.—as
the seven colors of the rainbow. Each color is independent and quite
able to stand alone with integrity. Yet together all make the rainbow.
There are individual theologies in the New Testament, and each one
has its own particular metaphors, symbols and models, together with
others which occur in more than one of the books. All the theologies
together, all the books, constitute the Word of God, the New Testament. So what we find there is a collection or cluster of models which
describe the relationship of the Christian and the Church to God—
sanctification, justification, reconciliation, forgiveness, regeneration
and so on. Each of these highlights one or another aspect of our
relationship with God and God's relationship with us. All together they
illumine the mystery of salvation, a reality which is not amenable to
final, literal description. Contemporary theology can take one or more
of these biblical models and interpret it/them in a way that makes sense
in the modern world. Or it can learn from that which all or most
highlight and illuminate and then on the basis of this knowledge

construct modern-day models which serve to highlight the same kind of meaning for today.

It will be very interesting to note whether the theme of justification once again becomes a powerful theological model in the churches for describing the relationship of God to the believer and the believer to God.

Notes

Chapter 1

1. For discussion of the theme of righteousness, see *The Interpreter's Dictionary of the Bible*, Vol. 4 and *Supplement*, Nashville, Abingdon, 1976. All the basic textbooks on Old Testament theology have sections on the topic—W. Eichrodt (two volumes, 1961, 1967), G. von Rad (two volumes, 1962, 1965), T. C. Vriezen (1958). The older works of J. Pedersen, *Israel* (four volumes, 1926, 1940) and N. H. Snaith, *The Distinctive Ideas of the Old Testament* New York, Schocken, 1944 are worth consulting. J. Barr, *The Semantics of Biblical Language* (1961) has helpful warnings about biblical word studies.
2. G. von Rad, *Old Testament Theology*, Vol. 1, New York, Harper & Row; Birmingham, England, SCM, p. 370.
3. *Op. cit., Interpreter's Dictionary*, Vol. 4, p. 80.

Chapter 2

1. See further D. Hill, *Greek Words with Hebrew Meanings* (1967); J. Reumann, *Righteousness in the New Testament* (1982); E. P. Sanders, *Paul and Palestinian Judaism*, Philadelphia, Fortress; Birmingham, England, SCM, 1977; and J. A. Ziesler, *The Meaning of Righteousness in Paul* (1972). The textbooks on New Testament theology all have sections on this theme—see those by R. Bultmann (1956), L. Goppelt (1982), J. Jeremias (1971) and W. G. Kümmel (1973).
2. The commentaries by H. D. Betz (1979) and F. F. Bruce (1982) on Galatians are excellent.
3. On these hymns, see J. T. Sanders, *The New Testament Christological Hymns* (1971) and E. Schweitzer, *Lordship and Discipleship* (1960).
4. The commentaries by E. Käsemann (1980) and C. E. B. Cranfield (1979) on Romans are excellent. See also M. Barth, *Justification: Pauline Texts Interpreted in the Light of the Old and New Testaments* (1971) and the provocative K. Stendahl, *Paul Among Jews and Gentiles*, Birmingham, England, SCM, 1977.

Chapter 3

1. Useful commentaries on James have been written by J. Adamson (1976), M. Dibelius (1976) and C. L. Mitton (1966).

Chapter 4

1. For the understanding of holiness with reference to the cultus, see J. Pedersen, *Israel,* Volumes 3, 4, pp. 198ff.; *op. cit.,* N. H. Snaith, *The Distinctive Ideas of the Old Testament,* pp. 21ff.; and O. R. Jones, *The Concept of Holiness* (1961). There are useful articles on holiness and sanctification in *op. cit., The Interpreter's Dictionary.*
2. See the article "Holy" and the literature cited in *The New International Dictionary of New Testament Theology,* Vol. 2, ed. Colin Brown, Grand Rapids, Zondervan, 1977; Exeter, England, Paternoster Press.
3. Compare Hans Küng, *Justification,* excursus 2 on "Justification and Sanctification," London, Search Press, 1964.

Chapter 5

1. Rainy, *The Delivery and Development of Christian Doctrine* (1874); see further P. Toon, *The Development of Doctrine in the Church,* Chap. 3, Grand Rapids, Eerdmans, 1979.
2. The latest appears to be Ben Drewery, "Deification," in *Christian Spirituality: Essays in Honour of Gordon Rupp,* ed. Peter Brooks, Birmingham, England, SCM, 1975.
3. For expositions of this later understanding, see V. Lossky, *In the Image and Likeness of God,* Crestwood, N.Y., St. Vladimir's, 1974 and John Meyendorff, *Christ in Eastern Christian Thought,* Chap. 6, Crestwood, N.Y., St. Vladimir's, 1975. Cf. E. L. Mascall, *Via Media,* Chap. 4, 1956, for a Western approach.
4. Cited by J. N. D. Kelly, *Early Christian Doctrines,* New York, Harper & Row, 1978; London, Black, 1968, p. 378.
5. *Ibid.,* p. 379.
6. The best study of Augustine is Peter Brown, *Augustine of Hippo,* London, Faber, 1967.
7. For the Pelagian controversy, see Gerald Bonner, *St. Augustine of Hippo: Life and Controversies,* Chaps. 8, 9, London, 1963.
8. The best is by John Burnaby, *Augustine: Later Works,* Library of Christian Classics, Vol. VIII, Philadelphia, Westminster, 1980.
9. *Ibid.,* Sec. 15, p. 205.
10. *Ibid.,* Sec. 18, p. 208.
11. See further Alister McGrath, "Justification—'Making Just' or 'Declaring Just,'" *Churchman,* Vol. 96, No. 1 (1982), p. 45. Augustine clearly stated that "the word 'justified' is equivalent to 'made righteous.'" See *op. cit.,* Burnaby, Sec. 45, p. 228.
12. *Op. cit.,* Burnaby, Sec. 15, p. 205.
13. Augustine, *Sermons,* Vol. 2, sermon 108, p. 781, in *A Library of Fathers* (1883).
14. *Op. cit.,* Burnaby, Sec. 65, pp. 249, 250.
15. *En in Psalm,* XLIV.2. I owe this reference and translation to Dr. McGrath.
16. *Op. cit.,* Burnaby, Sec. 18, 26, 49, pp. 208, 215, 233.
17. *Ibid.,* Sec. 15, p. 205.
18. *Ibid.,* Sec. 52, p. 236.
19. See the special pleading of James Buchanan, *The Doctrine of Justification,* Edinburgh, 1867, reprinted 1961, pp. 104ff. O. W. Heick, *A History of Christian Thought,* Vol. 1, p. 203 recognizes that Augustine is not a "Protestant" in this area and speaks of "a deplorable absence of an emphatic distinction between justification and sanctification. . . ."
20. Studies of Aquinas by F. C. Copleston (1955), E. Gilson (1957) and M. D. Chenu (1974) are profitable.
21. On the development of private penance see O. D. Watkins, *A History of Penance,* two volumes, London, 1920.
22. Editorial comment on p. 129 of *Summa* (Blackfriars edition), Vol. 30.
23. *De Gratia et Libero Arbitrio,* 17, in *Anti-Pelagian Writings,* Vol. 3, Edinburgh, 1876.
24. *Ibid.,* p. 6.

25. See H. A. Oberman, *Forerunners of the Reformation,* New York, 1966, and A. E. McGrath, "Forerunners of the Reformation? A Critical Examination. . . ," *Harvard Theological Review* (1982).

Chapter 6

1. For studies of Luther see R. H. Bainton, *Here I Stand: A Life of Martin Luther,* Nashville, Abingdon, 1978; London, New English Library, and James Atkinson, *Martin Luther and the Birth of Protestantism,* Atlanta, John Knox, 1981. For a very useful collection of documents see *Martin Luther,* eds. Rupp and B. Drewery, New York, St. Martin, 1970. The German edition of Luther's works is known as the *Weimarer Ausgabe.* There is an American edition, *Luther's Works,* in fifty-five volumes, St. Louis, Concordia.
2. See further P. Althaus, *The Ethics of Martin Luther,* Philadelphia, Fortress, 1972.
3. There is an English translation by J. I. Packer and O. R. Johnston, published in London in 1953 and often reprinted. Luther's book was aimed at refuting the views of Erasmus.
4. Cited by *op. cit.,* Bainton, p. 65. See also *op. cit.,* Rupp and Drewery, *Martin Luther,* p. 5.
5. See further the excellent chapter "The Problems of Luther's 'Tower Experience' and Its Place in His Intellectual Development," W. D. J. Cargill, in *Studies in the Reformation: Luther to Hooker,* London, Athlone Press, 1980.
6. For an exposition of Luther's doctrine see Paul Althaus, *The Theology of Martin Luther,* Philadelphia, Fortress, 1966, and Regin Prenter, *Spiritus Creator,* Philadelphia, 1953. In German see A. Peters, *Glaube und Work. Luther's Rechtfertigungslehre im Lichte der Heiligen Schrift,* Berlin, 1967.
7. There is a translation of these Articles in *The Book of Concord,* ed. T. G. Tappert, Philadelphia, Fortress, 1959, pp. 287-335.
8. *Op. cit.,* Althaus, *Theology of Luther,* p. 228, citing *Luther's Works,* 34, 153; 34, 178; 24, 347.
9. *Reformation Writings of Martin Luther,* two volumes, trans. B. L. Woolf, Vol. 1, New York, Philosophical Library, p. 363.
10. *Op. cit., Reformation Writings,* Vol. 2, pp. 288, 289.
11. *Op. cit.,* Althaus, *Theology of Luther,* pp. 227, 237, citing *Luther's Works,* 34, 152 and *Weimarer Ausgabe,* 39, 52.
12. *Ibid.,* p. 245, citing *Weimarer Ausgabe,* 39, 252.
13. *Op. cit., Reformation Writings,* Vol. 2, p. 289.
14. *Op. cit.,* Althaus, *Theology of Luther,* citing *Luther's Works,* 34, 151.
15. *Op. cit.,* Rupp and Drewery, *Martin Luther,* pp. 6, 7.
16. O. Pesch, "Existential and Sapiential Theology—The Theological Confrontation between Luther and Thomas Aquinas," in *Catholic Scholars Dialogue with Luther,* ed. Jared Wicks, Chicago, Loyola, 1970, p. 64ff.
17. Cf. B. A. Garrish, *Grace and Reason,* Chicago, University of Chicago Press, 1979, p. 133.
18. For studies of Melanchthon see R. Stupperich, *Melanchthon,* London, 1965; C. L. Manschreck, *Melanchthon: The Quiet Reformer,* New York, London, Greenwood, 1975; and M. Rogness, *Melanchthon: Reformer Without Honor,* Minneapolis, 1969.
19. For a translation of this see *Melanchthon and Bucer,* ed. W. Pauck, Library of Christian Classics, Vol. XIX, Philadelphia, Westminster, 1980, p. 3ff.
20. There is a translation of the *Augsburg Confession* in P. Schaff, *Creeds of Christendom,* Vol. 3 and of the *Confession* and *Apology* in *op. cit.,* Tappert, *The Book of Concord.*
21. *Op. cit.,* Pauck, *Melanchthon and Bucer,* pp. 88, 89, 105.
22. It has been suggested that Melanchthon gained his forensic understanding of imputation from reading the comments on Romans 4:3 made by Erasmus in his *Novum Instrumentum* (1516). See *op. cit.,* A. McGrath, "Justification—'Making Just' or 'Declaring Just.' "

23. R. S. Franks, *The Work of Christ*, London, 1962, pp. 324, 325.

24. See further Peter Fraenkel, *Testimonium Patrum: The Function of the Patristic Argument in the Theology of P. Melanchthon*, Geneva, 1961, pp. 32, 87.

25. There appears to be nothing of substance on Osiander in English. See, therefore, G. Sebass, *Das Reformatorische Werk des Andreas Osiander* (1967). F. Lau and E. Bizer, *A History of the Reformation in Germany to 1555*, 1969, pp. 230, 231, have some helpful comments on the controversy caused by Osiander.

26. The text is in Schaff, *Creeds*, Vol. 3 and in *op. cit.*, Tappert, *The Book of Concord*. The chief authors were Martin Chemnitz (1522-1586) and Jakeb Andreae (1528-1590). See also E. W. Gritsch, and R. W. Jenson, *Lutheranism: The Theological Movement and Its Lutheran Confessions*, Philadelphia, 1961 and W. Elert, *The Structure of Lutheranism*, St. Louis, Concordia, 1974.

27. See for details H. Schmid, *The Doctrinal Theology of the Evangelical Lutheran Church*, Minneapolis, Augsburg, 1961 and J. L. Gonzalez, "The Theology of Lutheran Orthodoxy," in *A History of Christian Thought*, Vol. 3, Nashville, Abingdon, 1975.

28. R. Preuss, "The Justification of a Sinner Before God," *Scottish Journal of Theology*, Vol. 13, No. 3, pp. 262ff. This article is primarily about Quenstedt's theology.

Chapter 7

1. The definitive study of the Council is Hubert Jedin, *A History of the Council of Trent*, two volumes, 1957, 1961.

2. *Op. cit.*, Jedin, *A History of the Council of Trent*, Vol. 2, p. 171.

3. For the canons and decrees in Latin and English see *op. cit.*, Schaff, *Creeds of Christendom*, Vol. 2.

4. A. von Harnack, *Dogmengeschichte*, Vol. 3, Tubingen, 1932, p. 711.

5. *Op. cit.*, Jedin, *A History of the Council of Trent*, Vol. 2, p. 309.

6. M. Chemnitz, *Examination of the Council of Trent*, Part 1, St. Louis, London, Concordia, 1971, p. 470.

7. *Ibid.*, p. 481.

Chapter 8

1. Of the many books on Calvin, that by F. Wendel, *Calvin*, London, Fontana, 1963, is most helpful.

2. The most recent translation of the *Institutes* is that by F. L. Battles in Volumes 20, 21 in the Library of Christian Classics (1961).

3. The Confession (1536) is found in translation in *Reformed Confessions of the Sixteenth Century*, ed. A. Cochrane, 1966.

4. The same order is found in the *Consensus Tigurinus* (The Zurich Agreement) made between Geneva and Zurich in 1549. It reads: "We are first accounted righteous . . . and are then regenerated. . . ." The text is in *Collectio Confessionum. . . ,* ed. H. A. Niemeyer, Leipzip, 1840, pp. 101ff.

5. On the role of divine election in Calvin's thought see *op. cit.*, Wendel, *Calvin*, Chap. 4, Sec. 4.

6. For the difference between medieval and Protestant definitions of faith, see Avery Dulles, S.J., "The Meaning of Faith. . . ," in *The Faith That Does Justice*, ed. J. C. Haughey, Mahway, N.J., Paulist Press, 1977, pp. 10ff.

7. Holmes Rolston, *John Calvin Versus the Westminster Confession*, Atlanta, John Knox, 1977.

8. For this argument see W. Cunningham, *The Reformers and the Theology of the Reformation*, Carlisle, Pa., Banner of Truth, 1979 and B. B. Warfield, *Studies in Theology*, 1932, p. 148.

9. See further Carl Bangs, *Arminius*, 1971 and P. Toon, *Puritans and Calvinism*, 1973, Chap. 6.

10. P. Toon, *The Emergence of Hyper-Calvinism*, 1967.

11. The first two are in *op. cit., Reformed Confessions,* ed. A. Cochrane, and all three are in *op cit., Creeds of Christendom,* Vol. 3.

12. See further R. T. Kendall, *Calvin and English Calvinism to 1649,* New York, London, Oxford, 1979 and the response to it from Paul Helm, *Calvin and Calvinism,* 1982.

13. See the very useful collection of material in H. Heppe, *Reformed Dogmatics,* Grand Rapids, Baker, 1950, reissued 1978. *Reformed Dogmatics* has selections from Johannes Wollebius, Gisbert Voetius and Francis Turretin.

14. *Op. cit.,* Heppe, *Reformed Dogmatics,* pp. 555-558.

15. J. Edwards, "Discourse on Justification by Faith Alone," in *Works,* two volumes, Vol. 1, Carlisle, Pa., Banner of Truth, 1979, pp. 622ff. Also, J. Owen, "The Doctrine of Justification by Faith," in *Works,* twenty-four volumes, Vol. 5, Carlisle, Pa., Banner of Truth.

16. See further S. E. A. Ahlstrom, "The Scottish Philosophy and American Theology," in *Church History,* Vol. 24, pp. 257ff.; and J. Vander Stelt, *Philosophy and Scripture: A Study in Old Princeton and Westminster Theology,* 1978.

Chapter 9

1. For Cranmer, see J. G. Ridley, *Cranmer,* 1962 and A. E. Pollard, *Thomas Cranmer and the English Reformation,* 1965.

2. For general background see N. S. Tjernagel, *Henry VIII and the Lutherans,* 1965, where there is a translation of the Articles. C. Hardwick, *A History of the Articles of Religion,* 1890, has the Latin text, pp. 259ff.

3. See P. Schaff, *A History of the Creeds of Christendom,* Vol. 1, 1877, pp. 343ff., 627-629 for the relation of the two statements of faith. There are also comments in E. Tyrell Green, *The Thirty-nine Articles. . . ,* 1896, W. A. Curtis, *A History of Creeds and Confessions of Faith,* 1911 and Peter Hall, *The Harmony of Protestant Confessions,* 1844.

4. It was held (e.g., by Gabriel Biel) that God was not bound to reward the sincere actions of unjustified sinners, but that it was fitting or congruous that he should do so. Thus the expression "grace (or merit) of congruity." Appeal was often made to God's acceptance of the prayers and alms of Cornelius before he truly believed (Acts 10:31).

5. A further interesting question is, What doctrine of justification is presupposed and/or stated in the two Prayer Books drafted primarily by Cranmer and printed in 1549 and 1552? There are many printings of the *Homilies,* but we lack a modern critical edition. The "homily on salvation" has recently been printed in P. E. Hughes, *Faith and Works: Cranmer and Hooker on Justification,* 1982.

6. This teaching of Melanchthon is found in the later editions of his *Loci Communes.*

7. See *Works of Thomas Cranmer,* Vol. 2, Parker Society, 1846, pp. 203ff. for evidence of this special study. The original is in Lambeth Palace Library.

8. Hooker has been the subject of much study recently; see J. E. Booty, "Richard Hooker," in *The Spirit of Anglicanism,* ed. W. J. Wolf, 1982.

9. See further C. F. Allison, *The Rise of Moralism: The Proclamation of the Gospel from Hooker to Baxter,* 1966.

10. The sermon is to be found in the Keble edition of Hooker's *Works* as well as in Vol. 1 of the Everyman edition of *Laws of Ecclesiastical Polity.* See also *op. cit.,* Hughes, *Faith and Works,* pp. 61ff.

11. Ireland was under the English crown at this time. These *Articles* apparently existed alongside the *Thirty-nine Articles* and were seen as an extension of their teaching. They are printed in C. Hardwick, *A History of the Articles of Religion,* Appendix VI, 1884.

12. For this controversy, see *Evangelical Theology, 1833-1856,* P. Toon, Atlanta, John Knox; Basing Stoke, England, Marshall Morgan and Scott, 1979.

13. See P. Toon and M. Smout, *John Charles Ryle,* Swengel, Pa., Reiner, 1976.

14. Cited by *op. cit.*, Allison, *The Rise of Moralism*, p. 141, from *Two Letters Written by the Rt. Rev. Thomas Barlow*, 1701.

15. Richard Baxter wrote *Aphorisms of Justification* in 1649. This caused controversy among Puritans. See *op. cit.*, Allison, *The Rise of Moralism*, p. 154 and *op. cit.*, P. Toon, *Puritans and Calvinism*, pp. 85ff.

16. Apart from Allison, see also J. W. Packer, *The Transformation of Anglicanism, 1643-1660*, 1969 and H. R. McAdoo, *The Structure of Caroline Moral Theology*, 1949.

17. P. Toon, "The Parker Society," *Historical Magazine of the Protestant Episcopal Church*, Vol. XLVI, No. 3, 1977.

Chapter 10

1. Recent biographies of Wesley include those by Martin Schmidt, two volumes, 1962 and A. S. Wood, 1967. Cf. F. Hillebrandt, *Christianity According to the Wesleys*, 1955.

2. W. R. Cannon, *The Theology of John Wesley*, New York, 1946, p. 63.

3. *The Journal of John Wesley*, ed. N. Curnock, eight volumes, Vol. 1, London, 1938, see February 1, 1738.

4. For pietism see F. E. Stoeffler, *The Rise of Evangelical Pietism*, Holland, 1965 and J. E. Hutton, *A Short History of the Moravian Church*, London, 1900.

5. *Op. cit.*, *Journal*, Vol. 1, under March 4, 1738.

6. *Ibid.*, under May 24, 1738.

7. *Sermons on Several Occasions*, London, 1944, Sermon 1, pp. 3, 4.

8. *Ibid.*, p. 6.

9. *The Works of John Wesley*, ed. T. Jackson, fourteen volumes, Vol. VIII, Grand Rapids, Baker; London, 1831, p. 284.

10. *Op. cit.*, *Sermons*, Sermon V, pp. 49-60.

11. See *op cit.*, Toon, *Puritans and Calvinism*, chap. 6 for the controversy.

12. *Op. cit.*, *Sermons*, Sermon XV, p. 174.

13. *Ibid.*, pp. 177, 178.

14. *Ibid.*, p. 178.

15. *Ibid.*, p. 182.

16. *Op. cit.*, *Works of John Wesley*, XIII, p. 9. H. Lindstrom, *Wesley and Sanctification*, 1950 is very helpful.

17. *Ibid.*, *Works*, XI, pp. 366-449.

18. This is well expressed in the hymns of Charles Wesley. See "The Promise of Sanctification," printed in *op cit.*, J. Wesley, *Sermons*, pp. 477-480.

19. See further D. W. Dayton, *The American Holiness Movement: A Bibliographic Introduction*, 1971 and H. V. Synan, *The Holiness-Pentecostal Movement*, Grand Rapids, Eerdmans, 1972. See also B. B. Warfield, *Perfectionism*, two volumes, Grand Rapids, Baker, 1931, 1932; R. N. Flew, *The Idea of Perfection in Christian Theology*, Atlantic Highlands, N.J., Humanities, 1934; W. E. Sangster, *The Path to Perfection*, 1943 and *The Pure in Heart*, 1954; G. A. Turner, *The Vision Which Transforms*, 1965; C. Williams, *John Wesley's Theology Today*, Nashville, Abingdon, 1972; and R. Brown, *Evangelical Ideas of Perfection*, Cambridge Ph.D. Thesis, 1964.

Chapter 11

1. The proof that Newman has been heard is seen in the ever continuing list of books about him that are published, by the moves to have him beatified and canonized, and by the number of times he is cited in recent Roman Catholic literature.

2. For the background to this, see *op. cit.*, P. Toon, *Evangelical Theology*, Chaps. 1, 5.

3. See further T. L. Sheridan, *Newman on Justification*, 1977.

4. John Henry Newman, *Justification*, 1838, p. 90.

5. *Ibid.*, p. 112.

6. *Ibid.*, p. 145.

7. *Ibid.*, p. 159.

8. *Ibid.*, p. 166.

9. *Ibid.*, p. 260.

10. *Ibid.*, p. 271.

11. *Ibid.*, p. 318.

12. Michael Schmaus, *Justification and the Last Things*, p. 22.

13. *Ibid.*, p. 34.

14. *Ibid.*

15. *Ibid.*, p. 35.

16. *Ibid.*, p. 63.

17. *Ibid.*, p. 72.

18. *Ibid.*, p. 73.

19. *Ibid.*, p. 110.

20. *Ibid.*, p. 115.

21. *Ibid.*, p. 141.

22. In *The Experience and Language of Grace*, Mahwah, N. J., Paulist Press; Dublin, Gill and Macmillan, 1979, R. Haight, S. J. looks at liberation theology as well as at the views of Karl Rahner. The latter has an article, "Questions of Controversial Theology on Justification," in *Theological Investigations*, Vol. IV, New York, Crossroad, 1966. See also Edward Schillebeeckx, "The Trindentine Decree of Justification," in *Concilium*, Vol. 5, 1965.

Chapter 12

1. Others whom I considered included Emil Brunner (see his *Dogmatics*), Helmut Thielecke (see his *Theological Ethics* and *The Evangelical Faith*), Reinhold Niebuhr (see his *Nature and Destiny of Man*) and T. F. Torrance (see his *Theology in Reconstruction*).

2. For Tillich's life and theology, see W. and M. Pauck, *Paul Tillich: His Life and Thought*, New York, Harper & Row; London, Collins, 1977. See also A. J. McKelway, *The Systematic Theology of Paul Tillich*, 1964.

3. Paul Tillich, *Systematic Theology*, three volumes, Vol. 3, Chicago, University of Chicago, 1973-1976, p. 237.

4. *Ibid.*, p. 242.

5. *Ibid.*, p. 246.

6. *Ibid.*, p. 247.

7. *Ibid.*, p. 249.

8. *Ibid.*, p. 251.

9. See David H. Freeman, *Tillich*, Phillippsburg, N. J., Presbyterian & Reformed, 1962 for a critical study of his view of God.

10. See J. C. DeMoor, *Towards a Biblically Theological Method: A Structural Analysis and a Further Elaboration of Dr. G. C. Berkouwer's Hermeneutic-Dogmatic Method*, Kampen, Holland, 1980.

11. See Berkouwer's *Studies in Dogmatic Theology*, Vol. 3: *Faith and Justification*, Grand Rapids, Eerdmans, 1954, pp. 26, 27.

12. *Ibid.*, p. 36.

13. *Ibid.*, p. 47.

14. *Ibid.*, p. 56.

15. *Ibid.*, p. 62.

16. *Ibid.*, p. 72.

17. *Ibid.*, p. 85.

18. *Ibid.*, p. 129.

19. *Ibid.*, pp. 137, 138.

20. *Op. cit.*, Vol. 1: *Faith and Sanctification*, 1952, p. 21.

21. *Ibid.*, pp. 66, 67.

22. *Ibid.*, p. 96.

23. *Ibid.*, p. 112.

24. *Op. cit.*, Berkouwer, Vol. 6: *Faith and Perseverance*, 1958, p. 79.

Bibliography

Biblical

Betz, H. D., *Commentary on Galations* (Philadephia: Fortress Press, 1979).

Brown, Colin, ed., *Dictionary of New Testament Theology* (Exeter & Grand Rapids: Paternoster & Zondervan, 1977).

Cranfield, C. E. B., *Commentary on Romans* (Edinburgh: T & T Clark, 1979).

Guthrie, Donald, *Theology of the New Testament* (Leicester & Downers Grove, IL: InterVarsity Press, 1981).

Käsemann, Ernst, *Commentary on Romans* (Philadelphia: Fortress Press, 1980).

Reumann, John, *Righteousness in the New Testament* (Philadephia: Fortress Press, 1983).

Ridderbos, Hermann, *Paul: An Outline of His Theology* (Grand Rapids: Eerdmans, 1977).

Sanders, E. P., *Paul and Palestinian Judaism* (Philadephia: Fortress Press, 1977).

Zeisler, J. A., *The Meaning of Righteousness in Paul* (Cambridge: University Press, 1970).

Historical and Contemporary

1. Primary

Aquinas, Thomas, *Summa Theologiae,* Blackfriars edition, Vol. 30 (London: Eyre & Spottiswoode, 1971).

Augustine of Hippo, "On the Spirit and the Letter," in *Augustine's Later Works,* J. Burnaby, ed. (Philadephia: Westminster Press, Library of Christian Classics, Vol. 8, 1980).

Berkouwer, G. C. B., *Faith and Justification* (Grand Rapids: Eerdmans, 1954).

Calvin, John, *Institutes of the Christian Religion* (Philadelphia: Westminster Press, Library of Christian Classics, Vols. 20, 21, 1980).

Cochrane, Arthur, ed., *Reformed Confessions of the Sixteenth Century* (Philadephia: Westminster Press, 1966).

Heppe, Heinrich, ed., *Reformed Dogmatics* (Grand Rapids: Baker, 1978).

Luther, Martin, *Three Reformation Treatises* (Philadephia: Fortress Press, 1960).

Newman, J. H., *Lectures on Justification* (London: Rivingtons, 1838).

Schaff P., ed., *Creeds of Christendom* (Grand Rapids: Baker, 1977).

Schmaus, Michael, *Dogma 6: Justification* (London: Sheed & Ward, 1977).

Tappert T. C. ed., *The Book of Concord* (Philadephia: Fortress Press, 1959)

Tillich, Paul, *Systematic Theology,* Vol. 3. (Chicago: University of Chicago Press, 1976).

Wesley, John, *Forty-four Sermons* (London: Epworth Press, 1956).

2. Secondary

Althaus, Paul, *The Theology of Martin Luther* (Philadephia: Fortress Press, 1966).

Bonner, Gerald, *St Augustine of Hippo* (London: SCM Press, 1960).

Cannon, W. R., *The Theology of John Wesley* (New York: Abingdon, 1946).

Haight, Roger, *The Experience and Language of Grace* (Mahwah, NJ: Paulist Press, 1979).

Kelly, J.N.D., *Early Christian Doctrines* (London: A & C Black, 1978).

Wendel, Francois: *Calvin* (London and New York: Wm. Collins and Harper & Row, 1963).

References to Holy Scripture

Index of Names and Topics